Beyond Politics

An Outline of Systematic Ideology

George Walford

gwiep.net 2021

Walford, George
[English]
Beyond Politics: An Outline of Systematic Ideology
ISBN 978-1-944651-23-7
1. Philosophy
2. Political Science
George Walford (1919–1994); Trevor Blake (b. 1966)

Publication history
1. London: Calabria Press 1990. 155 pages. Cloth.
2. Second Impression, Corrected. 155 pages. Paperback.
3. Columbus: gwiep.net. 232 pages. Paperback.

The George Walford International Essay Prize is an annual essay competition in memory of George Walford (May 1919 – August 1994). The subject of the essay is systematic ideology and the prize is £3,500 for the winner to spend at the college and on the course of the winner's choice. Everything necessary to apply for, research and win this Prize can be found at this website.

gwiep.net

127 House: At every turn in its thought society will find us waiting.

Contents

Publisher's Note

by Trevor Blake

GEORGE Walford published *Beyond Politics* in a hardcover edition in 1990. In that same year, he published a "second impression, corrected," as a paperback. In 1998 the book was transcribed for the internet. This is the first printed edition since 1990, and includes significant added material.

"Synopsis of Beyond Politics" (p. 171) is an undated and previously unpublished work discovered among the papers of George Walford. "Meet Systematic Ideology" (p. 175) was published in George Walford's journal *Ideological Commentary* in June 1994. "An Outline Sketch of Systematic Ideology" (p. 179) is a pamphlet published by George Walford in 1977. While George Walford intended *Beyond Politics* to take the place of the *Outline*, it is included in this edition to show how the theory has changed over time. The "Select Reviews" (p. 213) are gathered here for the first time. "Jack as I Knew Him" (p. 219) is by Alison Walford, Sharon Goodyer and Richenda Walford. It was first published in *George Walford, A Memorial (May 1919 – August 1994)*, edited by Trevor Blake and Richenda Walford.

As with the "Synopsis," a copy of *Beyond Politics* annotated by the author was discovered among the papers of the George Walford. These annotations are published here for the first time, as footnotes. The paragraph symbol (¶) is used to distinguish these newly-added footnotes from footnotes in the 1990 original. As George Walford wrote: "My ideas of today differ from those I held yesterday, one theory displaces another[1]."

The index has been expanded to include the new material, and to include publications (the original index included "persons, peoples and places").

This new edition of *Beyond Politics* has been proofread by, and made with the cooperation and support of Richenda Walford.

---

[1] p. 147

Beyond Politics

For Ike

Preface

IN 1977 I published a pamphlet, *An Outline Sketch of Systematic Ideology*, and in 1979 a book entitled *Ideologies and their Functions; a study in systematic ideology*. Since then systematic ideology has developed, and the present work is intended to take the place of those earlier efforts.

I have made contributions to the theory, especially in connection with the history of society at large and social activities outside party politics, but it is the creation of Harold Walsby (1911-1973). He worked in a line of descent that runs back through F. S. Johnson (to whom his *Domain of Ideologies* was dedicated), Francis Sedlak, the English Hegelians and Karl Marx to Hegel, and beyond Hegel to Kant and all the philosopher-predecessors, back to the woman, man or community who first attempted to make sense of their experience. Even that, as we shall see when we come to consider the evolution of ideology, is not the beginning of the line, but it is perhaps far enough to go in a preface.

My thanks are due to all who, knowingly or not, have helped hammer this book into shape; many an evening of knock-down, drag-out argument in the Anarchist Forum has gone into it. Much help, perhaps not always intentional, has come from the Socialist Party of Great Britain; without their demonstration of the limitations of other political movements, the stimulation provided by their determined opposition to systematic ideology, and the facilities for discussion so generously provided at their meetings, the theory could hardly have developed as it has. I have tried to reciprocate by drawing attention to their work.

One substantial advance beyond the earlier book is due to Ike Benjamin, who brought me to recognise the primal ideology for what it is. I am indebted to John Rowan for his detailed criticism of a late draft. My daughter Richenda read the proofs; my wife scrutinised the text and designed the jacket. This is beginning to sound as though everything in the book is owed to somebody else, but at least I can claim its defects for myself.

As this goes to print the reforms linked with Gorbachev's name are starting to produce their effects, including some to all appearance unexpected; the continued existence of the USSR, as my generation has known it, begins to look doubtful. When the lives of millions are being rapidly changed in ways closely connected with the theory to be presented there is a temptation to hold back and see what happens, but authors wanting their work to be taken seriously have to be willing to stick their necks out. For me this is easier than it might have been since recent events have moved in my favour, reducing an apparent discrepancy between social practice and the expectations deriving from systematic ideology.

Introduction

Books on ideology usually invite the reader to join the author in looking down, comfortably, on the antics of those suffering from the infection. Our approach will have to be more modest, for we shall find good reason to believe that ideology affects all of us and all our thinking, playing a part not only in failure, conflict and frustration but also in success, co-operation and progress.

This will come as less of a novelty today than it would have done even ten years ago, for ideology has begun to gain acceptance. But it has not yet become fully respectable and the study of it is seldom recognised as a distinct discipline. No university maintains a chair in ideology and the Subject Catalogue of the London Library lists nothing under this heading, referring the reader to philosophy, political science and social science. There is no agreed theory to account for the presence of ideology or to predict what effects it is likely to produce in future.

It was at the end of the Eighteenth Century that the term "ideology" first appeared, and in the Mid-Nineteenth that it came to be used in something approaching the modern sense, but it was not then that ideology began. Its effects can be traced, as we shall see, in the earliest human communities. Ideology has been present since thinking started, and the question whether it arises as cause or consequence of conditions of life is one we shall have to consider.

Zvi Lamm has divided the history of the study of ideology into three sections. The first of these began with the introduction of the term (in the French form) in 1796, and continued through Destutt de Tracy's *Éléments d'idéologie* of 1801-15 and the writing by Karl Marx and Friedrich Engels *The German Ideology* in 1845-6 to its publication in 1922, when the second, the classical, period began. In this the prominent landmarks are Lukacs' *History and Consciousness*, 1923, and Karl Mannheim's *Ideology and Utopia*, 1932. Lamm's third period began when the subject started to engage more academic attention in the early 1960s and is still

12

continuing[1].

Of the theories claiming to amount for ideology the only one to have made much public impact is that of Marx and Engels, presenting it as an influence imposing false consciousness upon the workers, dissuading them from revolution. The supporters of existing society were later to turn the concept against their critics, but not until the Mid-Twentieth Century did a work appear showing that ideology affects all purposeful behaviour. This insight was achieved by Harold Walsby. He started work in 1937 or 1938 – such undertakings rarely have beginnings which can be accurately dated – but spoke at first of psycho-politics, adopting the term ideology only in the mid-1940s and publishing his one book *The Domain of Ideologies*, in 1947. Since that date the word has come into general use, and the growth of interest in the subject which began in the early 1960s made it necessary for me to introduce, in 1976, the term systematic ideology to distinguish Walsby's theory from the rapidly growing number of others in the field.

The concept of ideology has served mainly as a political weapon, which is like using a computer as a club. Walsby's theory offers a more fruitful use, and one that extends far beyond the political arena, but he did come to it by the political route. As a young man in the 1930s he was attracted by the view that the answer to the difficulties being encountered by advanced industrial society lay in establishing common ownership and democratic control of the means of production, but he soon came to realise that the facts of social and political life did not agree with socialist theory and were not coming to do so. The socialists (and the communists too), believing themselves to represent the interests of the great majority against a dominant and exploitative minority, expected to receive overwhelming support. This had not been forthcoming, and the evidence did not show it to be any more likely than when the socialist movement had begun, over a century earlier. The great majority persisted in preferring their familiar way of life to the novelties offered them.

---

[1]Lamm 1984

The reformers and revolutionaries, or at least the more thoughtful ones, were of course aware of this discrepancy between their theory and the social realities. They ascribed it to the influence of the capitalists and argued that this was diminishing. They believed that as the contradictions of class society developed, and the people gained experience of its oppression, exploitation, warfare, misery and insecurity, they would realise where their true interests lay and come to support socialism or communism (or, at a minimum withdraw their support from capitalism, enabling these movements to operate). But Robert Owen, for whose work the word "socialism" was invented, had issued *The New View of Society* in 1813. The *Communist Manifesto* had appeared in 1848 and the first volume of *Das Kapital* in 1867. Decades had gone by, generations had lived and died, the centuries had begun to pass, and the new society had yet to appear. The bright hopes raised by the Russian Revolution had been trampled into bloody dust. In the absence of any predicted date for the socialists' victory it was still possible that their expectations might be realised, but it was becoming increasingly unlikely. Most of those who had been expected to provide the strength of the reformist and revolutionary movements persisted in supporting capitalism and the prospect of a collectivist economy attracted only a minority. Events of 1989 and early 1990, in the USSR, Eastern Europe and the People's Republic of China, have demonstrated that this is still so today.

Walsby rejected attempts to explain away the discrepancy between social reality and socialist expectations. He accepted the awkward fact, that people generally did not behave as these movements expected, and set out to examine the possibility that socialism might be not the expression in politics of the interests of the great majority but something else; the outcome of his work was the theory now known as systematic ideology. This explains how it comes about that there is no country in which the general body of the people subscribes to socialism or communism or anarchism. It also accounts for something less often recognised as needing explanation: the fact that in every advanced country each of these does enjoy a certain amount of support. Systematic ideology goes far to account for the presence of other political movements, their relative sizes and the degree of success or failure they encounter, but political activity is only a part of the behaviour it helps us to understand. It brings within one coherent system of thought, to name only three items, the facts that Democritus assumed his atoms to be indivisible, that the USSR and the People's Republic of China have moved towards official acceptance of competition and private ownership, and that policemen were invented before psychoanalysts.

Beliefs about the broader issues of politics, such as the desirability or otherwise of strong leadership, powerful armaments and a competitive economy, tend to come in sets, each of them with a group of people attached to it. These sets have come to be termed ideologies, and any general theory of ideology has to provide an explanation for them, for their presence and for their features. How does it come about that radically different ideologies appear within the one society? Are they restricted to political affairs or do they exercise a wider influence? Shall we have to reckon with them in future? We shall start our enquiry where the influence of ideology is generally recognised, in politics. In this area of activity, perhaps more than elsewhere, declared beliefs and intentions are sometimes difficult to reconcile with observed behaviour; this arises largely from interaction between different ideologies and we shall come to it later; at first I shall be speaking of each political ideology, and the effects it tends to produce, without taking into account its interaction with the others. After showing that there are grounds for carrying our thinking about ideology beyond the Marxist conception I shall sketch in the approaches adopted by the familiar political parties, drawing attention to features often regarded as secondary or even trivial and to their ideological implications. Then we turn to the influence of ideology in fields other than politics and in the history of society at large, finally investigating its origins and development. To begin with I shall speak indiscriminately of people having or holding ideas or beliefs, later examining these concepts more closely.

Discrepancies will sometimes appear between what I am saying and the results of direct observation, agreement being found only after analysis, but this is common in any serious study of an extensive field; many a hydrogen balloon has soared without disproving the law of gravitation. In the welter of daily politics one effect of ideology often interacts with another to produce confusing appearances, and the foreground is commonly taken up by events of the moment which divert attention from features more significant but less dramatic; Ben Hecht has remarked that trying to find out what is going on in the world by reading the newspaper is like trying to tell the time by looking at the seconds-hand. The influence of ideology appears most clearly in the long run and the broad outline, but we cannot rest there. In the long run we shall all be dead, and the broad outline has little to do with the price of whisky; if our work is to be of more than academic interest we shall also have to struggle with the difficulties of relating our results to life as we live it. We shall not be undertaking original research in the sense of discovering facts never known before, but rather bringing forward the significance of relationships, usually ignored or dismissed as unimportant, between events and phenomena familiar to every thinking person.

Walsby's work is unique among theories of ideology in that it accounts for theories of ideology, itself among them. In Lamm's words:

> its solution to the problem of the point of view
> from which one discusses an ideology is embod-
> ied within the theory itself, and does not require
> support from another historiographic theory, as
> is the case with Marx, or a sociological one, as
> with Mannheim[1].

That solution will appear as we go on.

---

[1]Lamm 1984

Politics as Ideology

L ATER on we shall need to look back to the beginnings of humanity, but now we turn to Western Europe in the middle years of the Nineteenth Century. By the mid-1840s Karl Marx and Friedrich Engels had begun to use 'ideology' in something approaching its modern meaning. They showed themselves aware of having broken through onto a new area of understanding, but a century and more of social development since their time has demonstrated that they did not recognise the full significance of their own perception. Throughout their work ideology remains secondary, an effect produced by class interests, although in later years Engels was according it a more active role than they did to begin with. Their original presentation appears in *The German Ideology*, written in 1845-6, and here they speak without hesitation; ideology consists of reflexes and echoes, it is bound to material processes, has no semblance of independence, no history, no development. Thinking and the products of thinking are not included in real existence. Explicitly, consciousness does not determine life[1]. If these things are so, then in order to understand ideology we need to study not ideology itself but the processes in the real world which it echoes, and continuing adherence to this belief by Marxists today explains why their studies said to be of ideology are seldom much more than accounts of class relations.

Marx and Engels were less rigid in their thinking. In 1890 (Marx had died in 1883) Engels was writing to Joseph Bloch expressing a view substantially different from the earlier one. The material or economic element no longer stands as the only determinant. Ideology is no longer seen as confined to reflexes and echoes, it has acquired history and development and become a part of real life, exercising a determining influence, sometimes even a preponderating one[2]. Three years later he had moved still farther in the same direction, condemning as fatuous the notion that he and Marx denied the ideological

---

[1]Marx and Engels 1970, 47
[2]Marx and Engels 1978, 436

sphere any effect upon history[1].

Even when *The German Ideology* was written there were grounds for questioning whether ideology could be adequately explained as a secondary effect of class interests, for some of the bourgeoisie, enough to demand mention even in the short *Communist Manifesto*, supported what Marx called the proletarian movement. Alvin Gouldner (describing himself as a Marxist outlaw), points out that from the viewpoint of Marx's and Engels' own theory the origination of that theory by "two very advantaged sons of the well-to-do" was a sociological miracle[2], and George Woodcock remarks the long line of aristocrats who joined the anarchist movement[3].

Since Marx's time the discrepancy between Marxist theory and social event has widened. In the *Communist Manifesto* he predicted that the proletarians, being a class, would come to form themselves into a party, but with the extension of the franchise those upon whom he bestowed this title have emulated the bourgeoisie and the aristocracy in spreading themselves over the political spectrum.

Down until fairly recent times "a party" did mean for the most part something close to what we would now call an interest-group; the great landlords of early Nineteenth Century Britain for example, became a party when they joined together to promote their common concerns. Parties as we know them today, mass organisations competing under conditions of universal franchise for control of the state, have other roots and serve other purposes, but the earlier meaning of the term still hangs on, bedevilling attempts to understand their behaviour.

Every movement big enough to be politically significant draws its numerical support mainly from the lower levels of the economic pyramid; in this they are all alike. But every one of them has its distinctive ideology. We have good grounds for entertaining the suggestion that in determining political attachment ideology may be the fundamental factor, class interest at most a minor influence.

---

[1] Marx and Engels 1978, 446
[2] Gouldner 1985, 7
[3] Woodcock 1963, 134

The main parties and movements fall readily into two groups, one comprising conservatism and liberalism, the other socialism, communism (used here to include Trotskyism and the other revolutionary socialist bodies) and anarchism. The first group, and particularly conservatism, is widely associated with the wealthy and powerful, the second with the ordinary people, the workers and the poor. Belief in these connections is so strong, and so widespread, that it would be surprising if there were no grounds for it, but it does present difficulties. There are only a few wealthy and powerful people; if they alone supported conservatism and liberalism, and everybody else the other movements, the socialist-communist-anarchist group would enjoy a permanent overwhelming majority, and this has not happened. Things fall into place when we accept that although the connection exists it is not a simple identity. Those who support conservatism and liberalism do not, for the most part, possess wealth or power themselves but they respect those who do, while to supporters of the other movements the presence of these things indicates oppression and exploitation.

The immediate distinction, between the members and supporters of one group of parties and movements and those of the other, lies not in possessions, income, status, or relation to the means of production but in ideas, views, beliefs, preferences, values and mental attitudes, in short in ideological features. We shall see later that this holds good also for the differences between individual parties and movements.

The Marxist view of ideology as false consciousness is by no means extinct, but the term has also come to be used objectively. When Roy Hattersley, Deputy Leader of the Labour Party, speaks in his book *Choose Freedom* of that party's ideology (and does so without provoking any fierce protest from its members) he clearly does not intend to suggest that its beliefs should be considered false. Nöel O'Sullivan who used "Conservative Ideology" in two chapter headings, and the other writers in the series published by J. M. Dent & Sons, *Modern Ideologies*, intend no disparagement. In 1947 Walsby was ahead of his time in using the term in this neutral way; following his example now we shall also be complying with a trend in current thinking.

One effect of the widespread influence of ideology is the tendency of political movements to talk past each other, using the same word for substantially different concepts. Conservative and liberal thinkers and writers tend to envisage workers as people doing rough or dull work for low pay, doubtless estimable but mostly not very bright, and needing supervision. In communist theory a worker does not suffer these limitations. Engels defined the working class as consisting of those obliged to sell their labour-power because they do not own enough to live without doing so[1], and used in this sense the term embraces most technicians, managers, professional people and administrators. One consequence of these differing interpretations is that to conservatives and liberals the idea of a society run entirely by workers appears absurd, while to those accepting Engels' definition it makes perfectly good sense. One group of purist anarcho-socialists (confusingly calling itself the Socialist Party of Great Britain and familiar to supporters and opponents as the SPGB) claim that the workers already run existing society 'from top to bottom[2].'

"Government," "profit," "conservatism," "socialism," "anarchy" (and many other political terms) also carry different meanings according to the movement using them. For anarchists government is the source of oppression, and communists see it as the executive committee of the ruling class, while for conservatives it represents the nation as a whole. Profit appears to conservatives and liberals as the reward due to those who run successful businesses, thereby providing jobs for the workers; reformers and revolutionaries see it as coming from exploitation. Conservatives see their movement as representing all that is truly British, while to their opponents it consists of a deluded mass supporting the interests of the wealthy few. Many anarchists envisage their favoured society as more orderly than any yet known, while to most non-anarchists the name of this movement suggests chaos. Using the same words for different concepts, the movements also use different words for the same thing. From 1917 up to

---

[1]Marx and Engels 1978, footnote to the English Edition of 1888
[2]SPGB 1969 20, 21

about 1990 the system operating in the USSR was socialism to communists, rabid Bolshevism to conservatives and state capitalism, oppressive and exploitative, to anarchists.

This diversity, exhibited by movements all inhabiting the one society (and all drawing their numerical strength mainly from people not distinguished by wealth or power) shows the meanings allocated to sensitive words to be powerfully influenced by something peculiar to each movement; the only factor capable of producing such an effect, and linked with all and only the members of each movement, is its ideology. Ideology affects political responses much as the nature of a surface affects the angle at which a ball rebounds from it.

In ordinary and academic usage "ideology" usually indicates a relatively superficial feature produced by something deeper (such as class interest, or psychological disposition), much as a surface ripple may be produced by a submerged rock. This approach minimises both the significance of ideology and the importance of ideological study. If an ideology is (intentionally or otherwise) adopted to further an inclination or to serve an interest then in order to understand it we need to study the inclination or the interest rather than the ideology, and those using this approach are right to devote the greater part of their attention to non-ideological factors. Systematic ideology takes the term in a deeper sense. Personality has little connection with ideology; Karl Marx and Mr. Gladstone were both dominant personalities but their respective ideologies differed radically. Rather than interests governing ideologies, ideologies determine interests, communists promoting (what they believe to be) working-class interests because of the beliefs they hold, rather than becoming communists because they are workers. Also, ideologies affect one another. By frustrating the socialists the attachment of the majority to existing society impels some of them towards communism; to a considerable extent, ideology determines ideology.

Evidence that ideology does influence behaviour, that it is not merely a collective term for ideas arising from non-ideological roots, comes from two familiar features of political activity. First, any attempt to achieve a thorough grasp of the beliefs which go to constitute a position tends to come after it has been adopted, committed anarchists studying anarchism committed liberals liberalism, and so on. Commitment to the ideology commonly comes before the accumulation of reason and evidence to justify it and largely decides which reasoning shall be considered sound, which evidence relevant.

Second, each political movement drives ahead along its chosen path without clear knowledge of where this may lead. This feature shows up best at the anarchistic extreme, where the SPGB make a point of asserting that the society they seek to establish does not exist and never has existed. It follows that their confidence in its virtues cannot be supported by direct evidence, but this does not trouble them. They require only that a majority should understand and accept what they say; given that, they would abolish present society, with its demonstrated ability to maintain the current world population, and replace it with their favoured system. They insist that for the change to be successful it must be complete, world-wide, and effected without any transition period. The conception allows no preliminary testing, no experiments, no pilot projects. Burning the bridges behind them, they would make the lives of five thousand million people dependent on a system without any direct evidence to show it workable. They claim to be scientific in their approach, but science advances tentatively, testing the ground at every step; the SPGB would advance to total reliance upon an untested social system in one megadeath-defying leap. The strength of their conviction is unquestionable, but it does not derive from experience of the condition advocated.

Communism, socialism and non-purist anarchism do not take this black-or-white approach, envisaging instead a period of transition between the old society and the new, a time of experimental advances, adjustments and, should they prove necessary, retreats. Pursuit of an object whose value has not been demonstrated in practice plays a smaller part in the activity of these movements but it still appears, for each step forward goes beyond what has been previously experienced, evidence of its viability coming (if at all) only after it has been taken. The same holds good, though to a lesser extent, even for conservatism and liberalism, for each of these also works towards an end which remains, in some respects at least, unknown until it has been attained. Experience shows that advances commonly do lead into new difficulties; the dangers we face from nuclear explosion and pollution, increase of population and damage to the environment arise from progress in particle physics, in public health and in technology. Much the same applies to attempts at returning towards traditional practices, for we live in a changing world and it is impossible to foresee just how the old methods, reinstated, would interact with the new conditions. Conservatism seeks to restore the police to the position it believes they once held in public esteem, but the Victorian bobby on his bicycle can find no place in a world of drugs, assault rifles and fast cars, and we have yet to find out what long-term effects the use of riot gear by the police is going to produce. No party has experienced exactly the condition it works to establish and consequently no party can provide empirical evidence that its proposals, put into practice, will not create difficulties worse than the ones they are intended to resolve. But this seldom gives the political movements pause; each of them pushes ahead, striving to bring social practice into accordance with its ideology.

Use of the phrase "an ideology" suggests that what is being spoken of is in some sense a unity, and common experience supports this; given one of the main ideas put forward by a party or movement not previously encountered it is often possible to predict, with a useful degree of reliability, which others will turn out to be associated with it. The broader political beliefs tend strongly to come in determinate sets, and this goes far to account for their notorious stability. Each of them being bonded to a set, trying to change it is like trying to pick up what appears to be a loose stone but is in fact the tip of a buried rock. An ideology possesses not only content but also enduring form and this helps to account for the persistence which shows through the shifting surface of politics. It helps to explain why the British Liberal Party survives (under a different name) although excluded from office for some seventy years and with no very evident prospect of returning and, on a larger scale, why the Russian communists persisted from 1917 to 1989 in the attempt to impose their ideas, and why dissidence survived under their repression.

Examination of the ideas making up an ideology shows them to be linked by something stronger than habitual association. Each political movement holds to a small number of extremely general propositions (we shall encounter some of them in the next chapter) and these change so slowly that when studying society (as distinct from pursuing absolute truth) they can well be treated as stable. Each movement's thinking consists, for the most part, of working out the implications of these broad beliefs in relation to changing circumstances, and its activity of trying to realise these implications in social practice, bringing the overall behaviour of society into agreement with its general ideas. We shall of course need to consider how these broad beliefs and general ideas arise, but that comes later.

The indications are that ideological behaviour forms a distinct category, closely related to psychology and, less directly, to physiology and anatomy, but not reducible to any or all of these without loss of its distinctive features. If we are to understand ideology it is not sufficient to study the conditions in which it arises; we must also study ideology itself.

Ideology exercises its influence for the most part in a diffused way and largely below the awareness of those affected. Its presence is an inference from observed behaviour and the most immediately relevant behaviour, that most directly linked to ideology, is the expression of ideas and beliefs. In the next chapter we shall look at some of the principal ideas and beliefs of the main political movements, and we shall find that they form a significant series, pointing to the presence, below the shifting political surface, of a stable ideological structure.

The British Political Series

WE turn now to the political scene in Britain, and not only because this is the country I know best. Britain, and particularly England, has enjoyed a greater freedom from disruptive external influences, over a longer period, than any equally advanced state; if there are regularities in the relationships between political parties they are likely to appear more clearly here than in countries where military, political or religious interference from without has played a larger part. (We shall go on to enquire whether regularities perceptible in Britain also appear in the greater world).

The immediate distinction between political parties and movements lies in their ideas, views, beliefs, preferences, values and mental attitudes, in short in ideological features. We begin by studying these, going on later to enquire how they come to hold the ones they do.

It may seem necessary to start by specifying the particular ideas held by the different movements, but this is not the best way to grasp their distinctive features. Particular ideas relate to particular circumstances and tend to change with them; they can provide no explanation for the enduring stability characteristic of major political bodies. Through much of the later Nineteenth Century, and the first half of the Twentieth, the British Empire bulked large in conservative thinking; now the empire has gone, and many conservative ideas with it, but conservatism remains recognisably what it was, and this because its ideology comprises not only particular ideas about particular issues but also certain broad beliefs. These endure while the particular ideas come and go and the same holds good, with appropriate changes, for the other movements. To be a conservative, a liberal or whatever, is to accept certain general ideas which govern responses to particular issues as they arise, and we shall study mainly ideas of this type.

Enthusiasts of every colour tend to reject any suggestion that systematic relations obtain between political movements. They like to select their own as right and dismiss all others as wrong, and this is like saying that all animals are either elephants or not elephants; true or not, it obscures a lot of useful information. There are good grounds for holding that the principal British political movements form an orderly sequence, and we shall find as we go on that this indicates the presence of a firm ideological structure beneath the ever-changing political surface.

Size and Influence

Each movement exercises upon social life a degree of influence immediately determined mainly by the number of people supporting it. Millions, rich and poor, accept conservative ideas and the movement is correspondingly powerful not only at the polls but also in less formal ways; the economic and political systems of modern Britain operate largely in accordance with conservative beliefs and have continued to do so when the Conservative Party was out of office. Anarchist ideas appeal to far smaller numbers, and this movement exercises so little influence that even a detailed history of modern Britain would be likely not to mention it. When these two movements are taken as the ends of a range and the others inserted between them to produce a series running: conservatism, liberalism, socialism, communism, anarchism then, consistently over the whole range, a movement tends to be large and powerful, or small and ineffective, as it stands closer to one extreme or the other.

Apparent exceptions lose much of their substance when examined. The Labour Party has repeatedly obtained enough electoral support to form a government, while the rule places socialism among the smaller movements; the explanation lies in the distinction between the party and the movement. Most of the numerical and financial strength of the Labour Party comes from its trade union component, and this for the most part is markedly non-socialist; a trade union works to promote the interests of its own paid-up members rather than the welfare of the working class or the community, it equates with the cartels, price-rings and attempted monopolies of management and employers.

During the last two decades of the Nineteenth Century, before the trade unions and the socialists came together in one party, the numerical disproportion between the two groups showed up clearly. The principal socialist organisation of the time, the Democratic (later Social Democratic) Federation had a membership in the hundreds for most of this period, and by 1900 had reached only ten thousand, while already by 1890 the trade unions counted 1,600,000. The difference in ideas between the two groups also showed up; when the Federation issued a manifesto to the trade unions it succeeded only in alienating them. The movement to substitute a new form of society for the existing one gained little strength in later years; in his 1965 history of the Labour Party Brand notes that under nationalisation "the professional managers were concerned with efficiency rather than socialism, and the structure of British industry remained essentially capitalist[1]," and Neil Kinnock, Leader of the party, told the 1988 Conference that its job was the efficient operation of capitalism[2]. Socialism was a minority influence within the Labour Party at its foundation and has remained so; it is a relatively small and weak movement.

Another discrepancy, between our rule and the results of observation, shows up when we recall that since the early 1920s liberalism has consistently held a smaller number of parliamentary seats than its position in the range would lead one to expect; this results largely from Britain's electoral system. I am using "liberalism" to include what is known in British politics as social democracy, and if seats won in the 1987 General Election had been in proportion to votes cast the Alliance (of the Liberal and Social Democratic parties) would have won 146 seats instead of the 22 actually held[3].

Provided the distinction between socialism and the Labour Party be maintained, and we look at votes cast rather than seats won, electoral results tend to support our proposition: the farther along the range towards anarchism each movement stands, the smaller its size and influence. (When we come to look beyond Britain we shall find the striking apparent exceptions in Russia, China and elsewhere also falling into

---

[1] Brand 1965, 1-12, 246
[2] Samizdat November 1988
[3] *New Statesman* 24 July 1987, *Guardian* 11 June 1987

place upon closer examination. As I write, early in 1990, these discrepancies are weakening, but they remain marked enough to need accounting for).

From Stability to Revolution

Next we ask whether this diminution in numerical support along the range can be shown to correspond with differences in ideas or beliefs, and I take first the degrees of enthusiasm which the parties respectively show for far-reaching changes in the deep structures of society. Conservatives tend to value the established, priding themselves on being responsible people, too sensible to abandon what has been proven viable in a chase after perfection. Liberals, while working for radical changes, yet seek to perfect existing society rather than replace it by something fundamentally different. Socialism, communism and anarchism, on the other hand, all advocate transition to a society operating on different principles. When we enquire more closely, taking each movement by itself, we find that here also our series holds good; the nearer to anarchism a movement or party stands, the deeper and more extensive the changes sought.

To say that conservatism seeks to preserve things as they are would be going much too far; conservative governments pass laws and conservative ministers issue regulations, and every one of these constitutes a change. Conservatism does, however, maintain a distinctive attitude towards changes, promoting only those which (it believes) will tend to avert greater ones. Placing high value on stability, conservatism conceives it to be threatened and is prepared to put up with much, even with extensive changes, in order to secure it.

In liberalism this alters; change comes to be valued as a means towards positive benefits. Nostalgia no longer tempts, the ideal has yet to be achieved. Still holding firmly to the main features of existing society, such as its authoritarian government and competitive economy, liberalism differs from conservatism in seeking rather to perfect than to preserve them, aiming at progress rather than stability. The recommendations of J. M. Keynes for manipulation of the economy to avoid the recurrence of booms and slumps, and the work of

Sir William Beveridge in softening the harsher edges of capitalism, provide large-scale examples of the approach. Where conservatism sometimes holds back from the correction of abuses or malfunctions, fearing that interference may produce a condition worse than before, liberalism seeks out opportunities for improvement. It prefers to confine itself, however, to the improvement of what already exists, Bentley noting that Hobson agreed with all liberals of all periods in seeing nothing amiss *in principle* with capitalism, believing that it was for government to ensure that it worked in a wholesome way[1].

With the next step along the range, to socialism, attention shifts from separate improvements to the reformation (re-formation) of society from the roots up. Here common ownership and co-operation are to replace private ownership and competition, and a government more responsive to the people is to displace the present system of authority tempered by occasional elections. These objectives of socialism are often summarised, in a phrase significant for our enquiry into the degrees of change favoured by the different movements, as the *alternative* society.

Moving on past socialism, communism comes to value radical change highly enough to undertake revolution in order to effect it, and anarchism believes it not enough even to revolutionise existing society, proclaiming the only way of overcoming its defects to be its abolition, leaving people free to follow their inherent leanings towards peaceful cooperation.

When arranged according to the depth and extent of the changes they favour the movements fall into the same order as when listed by size. This suggests that the arrangement expresses real relationships between them and as we go on to look at other features we shall find this impression strengthening into a virtually unavoidable conclusion. I shall take their ideas about control versus freedom, first in economic and then in political affairs, and go on to look at the differing valuations they respectively place upon theory as a guide to action.

---

[1]Bentley 1987, 92, emphasis in the original

Economics: from Freedom to Control

Each of our movements declares itself in favour of freedom, and each of them is found on examination to understand by the term a particular set of restraints (which we are about to specify). In addition to these specialised meanings, each of them confined to a certain group, the term is used in two senses which come close to being opposed. They are often distinguished as "freedom to" and "freedom from," and I shall use the word in the first sense, meaning freedom to act, not freedom from the consequences of action. The difference will become clearer as we go on.

Willingness to allow individuals freedom of action in economic affairs, freedom to buy, to sell to accumulate possessions or to fail to obtain what they need (according to their ability, industry, cunning, avarice or good fortune), is strongest in conservatism. This movement does impose restraints upon economic competition, requiring that participants act honestly, legally and decently – in a famous phrase, that they present an acceptable face – but these requirements leave competition free to the point where the victors are able largely to exclude the losers from the field, leading to its domination by the multi-nationals, conglomerates and the like.

Liberalism would not allow competitive individualism this free rein. Liberals often speak and write as if they sought unrestricted competition but in fact government control plays a larger part in their preferred economy than in that of conservatism. The proposals of both Keynes and Beveridge entailed tighter management of the economy than conservatism willingly undertakes, and when Michael Bentley likens a liberal economy to a cricket match[1] his choice of simile is unintentionally revealing, for cricketers perform under an elaborate system of rules imposed by unquestionable authority. Bentley recognises that for the game to take place the pitch has to be kept clear; exploitation, monopoly, unfair advantage, corruption and bigotry must be suppressed. By calling these practices artificial he sets up fair competition as the normal or natural condition and this puts things the wrong way round.

---

[1]Bentley 1987, 987, 40

A pitch *with obstructions* displays the normal or natural state of such areas; the clear and level one is the artificial construction. Exploitation, monopoly and the rest have been with us since structured society first appeared, maintaining themselves against all attacks, and to speak as if getting rid of them were no more than a preliminary clearing of the ground reminds one of the plan for a robbery that began: "First, you steal a battleship." A government capable of ensuring that the individual shall encounter only free and fair competition would be no distant umpire but a pervasive presence, powerful enough to overcome any combination of opponents. In practice liberalism tends to accept this, the freedom it envisages being largely that provided by a powerful state and a government less inclined than are conservative ones to permit an economic free-for-all; in partly dismantling the Welfare State the Thatcher government acted without support from liberalism.

Socialism would regulate industry and commerce more closely still seeking to subordinate competition and private interests to the welfare of the collectivity. Here the economic system which produces all wealth, is held to be operated not by individuals but by society, and people who enjoy plenty while others, equally members of society, suffer poverty, are seen as taking things to which they have no moral right. During periods of Labour government the socialist impulse in the party has brought monopolies and near-monopolies under direct government control and extended supervision to privately-owned enterprises. Where conservatism aims at leaving citizens to decide for themselves how to spend what money they have, socialist influence in the Labour Party leads it to seek rather to make these decisions for them, imposing heavy taxation (especially but not exclusively upon the rich) and using the proceeds to provide uniform services for all. In the economic field, in activities connected with material goods and buying and selling, socialism would regulate behaviour more closely than either liberalism or conservatism. The famous Clause Four of the Labour Party's Constitution (ignored by the non-socialist bulk of its members) shows socialism committed to common ownership and democratic control of the means of production, and to the extent that these are instituted individual freedom of action in this sphere diminishes.

With the next step, to communism, the demand for common ownership hardens; the socialist conviction that restraints must be imposed only gently and gradually is rejected, and the degree of economic control envisaged becomes so severe that even its proponents speak of a dictatorship (of the proletariat).

This may sound as though control has reached its limits, but in the society favoured by anarchists it would become even more severe, going indeed beyond control or even suppression of independent economic action towards its elimination. Dictatorship, with its coercive apparatus, implies the presence of substantial resistance; were no considerable body striving to exercise freedom, these powerful means of suppression would not be needed. In an anarchist society they would be superfluous, informal action by the community being sufficient, and this indicates the degree to which impulses towards independent economic action would have to be eliminated for such a society to function.

The picture of an anarchist economy as leaving people free to make and to do whatever irresponsible fancy may suggest, each of them acting independently, is one not held by serious anarchist thinkers. Daniel Guérin quotes Bakunin as advocating workers' co-operatives which would be organised as one enormous federation, with a single assembly in supreme control. Using precise, detailed and comprehensive world-wide statistics it would maintain correlation between supply and demand, directing, distributing and sharing out the industrial production of the world; in this way losses of capital, stagnation, crises of employment and trade and other economic disasters would almost certainly, Bakunin believed, entirely disappear[1]. The idea of a body which should balance supply and demand, worldwide, in all fields, stands out as a hold conception even in an age of computers. To propose it well before the end of the Nineteenth Century (Guérin does

---

[1]Guérin 1970, 55

not detail his sources but Bakunin died in 1876) shows an enthusiasm for control in economic affairs fully equal to the ardour with which conservatives demand freedom in this field.

This also supports another of our themes. Bakunin is well known as an opponent of Karl Marx; when, in spite of this, his economic proposals turn out so close to the ultimate aim of the communists, it goes to confirm that anarchism is best understood as a step beyond communism rather than as a movement arising from separate roots, even though anarchists themselves often repudiate any suggestion of significant connection between the two.

Politics: from Control to Freedom

Turning to political-intellectual activities, we find the tendencies displayed in the economic-material field reversed; here conservatism and (to a lesser extent) liberalism favour regulation while socialism, communism and anarchism, in that order, favour increasing degrees of individual freedom. The *strength of the commitment* to economic-material *freedom displayed by each movement varies inversely with its commitment* to political-intellectual freedom.

Conservatism holds that authority should control education, restrain agitations and demonstrations, impose restrictions on public speech and the press, strengthen the powers of the police and extend the remit of the security services. When in power it tends to follow this course and to make no apology for doing so, for this is how its supporters want it to behave. In its internal organisation it follows the same pattern, the leaders exercising greater authority, and the general body of members a less active influence, than in any of our other movements. Strongly supportive of individual enterprise in economic matters, conservatism discourages it in political and intellectual affairs, stressing instead the value of loyalty and conformity[1]. The Thatcher regime has enthusiastically pursued deregulation of economic life together with the imposition of greater State control over teaching and research.

Liberalism modifies these views, holding the correct attitude in political and intellectual affairs to be not the reduction

---

[1]Gilmour 1977, 151-167

of differences of opinion but encouragement of them so far as may be consistent with the security of the state, and Liberal Assemblies tend to carry this theory into practice. They are inclined, noticeably more than Conservative Conferences, to pass resolutions going against the policies favoured by their leaders. This tendency, like others, gets carried farther in the next step along the range; Tony Benn tells us that "the Labour Party feels free to be critical of everything the leader says and does... [1]" and it is particularly the socialists within that party who take advantage of this freedom.

Among communists mental independence reaches a point where severe party discipline has to be imposed to make it possible to maintain a functioning organisation, and even so the movement exists mainly as a collection of fragments expending much of their energy in fighting each other, while anarchists not uncommonly deny that they constitute a movement at all, claiming to be nothing but a number of fully autonomous individuals.

I have been speaking of individual freedom of action in political matters as it appears in the behaviour of the people making up each movement; it also appears in the behaviour of the movements themselves, and here again it shows the same progression, each movement asserting its independent individuality more strongly as it stands closer to anarchism.

Conservatism deprecates any suggestion that it engages in party-political action, claiming to represent the nation as a whole, and each conservative prime minister since Peel (with the exception of Douglas-Home) has formed, attempted or considered a coalition with other parties[2]. At the other end of the range the purist anarchists of the SPGB declare themselves "determined to wage war with all other political parties[3]" and have in fact never allied themselves with any other political movement (save for companion-parties abroad) since the foundation of their party in 1904.

In moving along the range from conservatism towards anarchism the degree of political-intellectual freedom of action

---

[1] Benn 1982, 34
[2] Gilmour 1977, 65
[3] Socialist Party of Great Britain, Principle No. 8

demanded and exercised, both by the successive movements and by the people within them, consistently increases. In respect of this feature, also, the movements fall into the same order as before.

Theory: from Scepticism to Confidence

I will take one more feature in confirmation: the valuations the movements respectively place upon theory as a guide to action. Conservatism sets this low. Sir Ian Gilmour has a chapter entitled "Conservative Philosophy," but any idea that this may indicate high valuation of theory disappears on reading its opening sentences:

> So far, then, as philosophy or doctrine is con-
> cerned, the wise Conservative travels light. Con-
> servative principles cannot be precisely tabu-
> lated. To ask what is the nature of Conser-
> vatism is more to the point than to seek to
> categorise it.

He adds that "Conservatives are more concerned with life than with theory," and that "it is the function of Tories to bring common sense to bear, to look at theory in the cold light of practice, to scrutinize ideals and schemes with great care... "; he goes on to say that from Hume conservatives get "scepticism, the sense of the falliability of human reason," and from Burke "the love of the concrete and the hatred of abstraction[1]." This is the orthodox conservative view, supported by other writers. John Burrows for example notes the incongruity of expressing conservative ideas in declaratory or abstract terms, saying they are better exhibited, to use Stubbs' metaphor, in solution; embodied, and absorbed one instance at a time. They fit better into the writing of history than into theoretical exposition[2].

Adherence to what experience has proven viable, reluctance to go adventuring after strange theories, sound as dominant notes in conservative thought, and Disraeli adds his barbed

---

[1]Gilmour 1977, 109, 169, 170
[2]Burrow 1981, 131

comment: "We must remember that this country is not governed by logic, but by Parliament[1]."

Liberalism allows theory a more prominent role, taking its philosophy straight and recognising the Philosophical Radicalism of Bentham and others as one of the sources from which it sprang. The movement has been described, by the editors of one collection of extracts from liberal writers and speakers, as "a set of ideas[2]," a phrase conservatives, preferring to be guided by "traditional manners of behaviour" and "balance, prudence and moderation[3]," would not welcome as a description of their beliefs. A concern with ideas, rather than with the tradition, principle and character stressed by conservatives, tends to play a prominent part in accounts of the roots of liberalism. Michael Bentley, for example, comments on the formative role which liberalism ascribes to the power of thought and the ideas and values of intellectuals, and speaks of liberalism as "a bundle of recognisable and persistent ideas," "a set of doctrines that float above the party melee." He speaks of a "thought-world" inhabited by liberal intellectuals, and of J. S. Mill holding that a properly conceived system of representative government would introduce an intellectual test for electors[4]. This movement shows a marked shift away from the firm practicality of the conservative approach and towards theorisation. Emphasis upon this distinction was a feature of the long struggle of the two parties through the late Nineteenth and early Twentieth Centuries, conservative writers repeatedly accusing liberalism of being so committed to rigid theories as to have lost pragmatic flexibility.

From some of the viewpoints available today this difference between conservatism and liberalism looks like hardly more than a shift of emphasis; the next step brings a more substantial change. Unlike liberalism, socialism accepts only provisionally the private ownership, nationalism and status differences of existing society, and in seeking to move forward to a new earth, if not also a new heaven, it relies upon theory

---

[1]Doolittle, quotation on title-page.
[2]Bullock & Shock 1967, xxiiv
[3]Gilmour 1977, 110-111
[4]Bentley 1987, 42, ix, xviii

to show the route. At this point in the series theory comes to be valued above experience as a guide to action. Liberal ideas are still closely related to practical problems, retaining something of an *ad hoc* quality, but socialism tends to relate all the major social problems to the single root of institutionalised inequality, and this endows its thinking with a new coherence.

Communism launches out more boldly. Already in 1848 Marx was crediting the communists with an understanding of social affairs superior to that of the general proletariat[1], and Lenin follows suit, insisting on the vanguard party's need of the most advanced theory and driving his point home: "without communist theory, no communist movement[2]." Here theory is valued so highly that even violent revolution is acceptable to bring practice into agreement with it, and the theorising itself is of a quality not found in the movements spoken of above. Liberalism concerns itself with ideas, but the thinking found in Michael Bentley's chapter on theory, or even in Mill or Keynes, is eminently down-to-earth and practical when compared with Marx's *Das Kapital*, Engels' *Anti-Duehring*, or even the comparatively popular *Communist Manifesto*. While conservative, liberal and (with few exceptions) also socialist writers maintain close contact with their audience Marxist intellectuals, for all their professed concern with those who have not enjoyed advanced education, often ascend into a stratosphere where few can follow them.

---

[1] Marx & Engels 1978, 62
[2] Lenin 1973, 29, 28

Michel Pecheux, for example, complains that the material conditions of capitalism disrupt communication between the workers and the control of production. In communicating his own ideas he says:

> interdiscourse as transverse discourse crosses and connects together the discursive elements constituted by interdiscourse as preconstrued, which supplies as it were the raw material in which the subject is constituted as speaking-subject, with the discursive formation that... tends to absorb-forget interdiscourse in intra-discourse... [1]

In anarchism the action advocated comes to be guided by theory almost to the exclusion of experience. Every society producing its own food has used authority and coercion; these have varied in form and extent, but no society with a population greater than the few who could live off natural growth has survived without them. Socialism and communism, although intending to impose great restrictions on the use of these methods, and to turn them to purposes to which they have not yet been applied, yet remain free to use them without falling into fatal self-contradiction; there is to be no complete break between existing society and what they advocate, they have achieved some of their minor objectives and it remains to be discovered by experiment how much farther it is possible to move in the direction they wish. Anarchism cannot act in this way. Defining itself as the absence of authority and coercion it can claim no practical successes to demonstrate the validity of its theorising. The apparent success of anarchism in Spain in the 1930s was deceptive[2] and the communes, co-operatives and so on sometimes offered as evidence for the practicality of anarchist proposals are nothing to the point since they all functioned within an authoritarian environment. There is no direct empirical evidence at all to support the feasibility of a self-sufficient anarchist society and while this

---

[1] Pêcheux 1983. I cannot claim to have read this book; the quotation comes from the *TLS* September 30th 1983

[2] see Appendix A, p. 161

does not, of course, prove such a society impossible, it does mean that those who work to bring it about do so in reliance upon theory, without direct support from exprience. Guérin quotes the observation of Diego Abad de Santillán that anarchism "had produced a super-abundance of works, in every language, going over and over an entirely abstract conception of liberty[1]."

When arranged according to their conception of the relative values of theory and experience as guides to action, the movements fall into the same order as before.

The Non-Political Group

The range of movements now on the table comprises the main active constituents of British political life but not the whole population or even the whole electorate. At each British general election this century some twenty per cent have refrained from voting (in 1987 the figure was 24.6 per cent), while swings and landslides indicate the presence of a body of voters without firm party commitment, a body large enough, when many of them move in the same direction, to sway the result. Doubtless some of the non-voters are anarchists, or others who have analysed the policies on offer and reached a considered decision that no party deserves their support, but such people are rare. Through any political excitement the great majority, rich and poor, educated and uneducated, carry on as if nothing were happening; even the largest demonstration loses its impressiveness when one thinks of the numbers who have preferred to stay at home or at work. The proportion of "Don't knows" reported by each survey of political opinion, the complaints, from activists of all parties, of widespread apathy, and the contacts we all make in everyday life indicate that the largest group of all consists of those not identified with any party or movement. For the most part these people ignore elections, and when any of them do cast a vote it is guided by considerations other than adherence to any set of political principles. The indications are that most of the non- voters, and the "floating" voters too, take little or no thoughtful interest in politics; they vote for this or that party,

---

[1] Guérin 1971, 134

or stay away from the polling-booth, as they think will best serve their interests at the time, and I shall call them the *non-politicals.*

The movements discussed above all seek to modify society. Conservatism seeks less radical change than any of the others but it, too, works to bring social practice into agreement with its beliefs, seeking to ensure that wealth and status shall be enjoyed and payment, profit and perquisites pursued, within the conventional decencies. Seen from positions closer to anarchism, with their more severe restraints upon individual enterprise, this may not seem very much, but the non-politicals do not limit themselves even to that extent. In economic affairs they are less influenced by a regard for the common welfare, more individualistic, than conservatives. This does not have to mean they will behave rapaciously, and in fact the demands made by most of them even in the wealthiest countries tend to be remarkable for their modesty. It means they are free to follow their personal inclinations unencumbered by any burden of doctrine. Emotional responses may lead them to behave towards people, even in the mass, with generosity and sometimes with self-sacrifice, but there is nothing in their beliefs committing them to act with considered regard for anything so remote as a nation or a class; that comes with the beginnings of intellectualisation and an extension of interest from personal concerns to the political arena.

Turning from the economic field to the political, here again the non-politicals show themselves by their behaviour to be standing farther from anarchism than conservatism does. By being sceptical of theory conservatism shows awareness of it, and the non-politicals have not got as far as that; the possibility that theory might influence action hardly enters their thinking even as a risk to be guarded against. Conservatism deplores efforts to promote any sectional or party viewpoint, stressing the importance of national unity; in doing that it takes up a definite stand, while the non-politicals remain as the politically featureless background from which it distinguishes itself. Conservative principles have repeatedly led their adherents to demand war but the non-politicals rather emulate Auden's Unknown Citizen, favouring peace in times of peace but obedient when ordered out to fight. Within broad limits they accept society as it is, adapting themselves to it rather than seeking to bring it into line with any more or less coherent set of ideas. Not perceiving politics as an area in which ends are to be pursued they see no need for any freedom of action in the field and accordingly are not brought to protest, as some conservatives are sometimes driven to do, that the political control imposed by government is becoming oppressive. These people constitute the largest group of all and hence the one exercising the greatest influence. Abstainers from voting and uncommitted voters as they are, their numbers none the less have the effect that it lies mainly in their hands to decide which party shall hold office and the main outlines of the course to be followed. What they are willing to accept sets the limits within which the parties work. By their size and influence, as well as by their beliefs, they locate themselves at the end of our series as a sixth term out beyond conservatism.

Each of these six groups exhibits five features, namely size, changes sought, preference for freedom or control in economic and political affairs respectively, and value placed upon theory as a guide to action. When the groups are arranged in the order: non-political, conservative, liberal, socialist, communist, anarchist, then each feature changes consistently right along the range and these systematic relationships do not appear, with features of comparable importance, if they are arranged in any other way. For one feature to change in this way between two groups would mean little, and two features changing over a range of three groups might well be an effect of chance. But when five major features change consistently over the whole range it comes close to being proof that this arrangement of the parties and movements of which we have been speaking expresses real and significant relationships.

The World Political Series

THE British parties do not appear in the rest of the world and verbal correspondences are usually misleading. The Bolsheviks originated as one wing of the Russian Social Democratic Party, but this does not make a British social democrat a Bolshevik (or a Menshevik either), and an American liberal is not the same as a British one. The British parties possess features peculiar to themselves, and so do those of every independent state, but in their more substantial features the major ones link up, none the less, with political regularities extending throughout the advanced world. The three broad classes into which the principal British groups fall – the non-politicals, the defenders and improvers of existing society, the reformists and revolutionaries – appear in all advanced countries (proportional representation tends to increase the number of organisations into which each political category is divided) and they everywhere exhibit substantially the same features and relationships as in Britain.

The rule, outside Britain as within, is that the greater the changes one of these political classes seeks to achieve the smaller its size and, consequently, the weaker its influence. The consistency with which this obtains is not self-evident; trouble makes news, and it takes an effort to remember the millions living peacefully behind the upheavals that fill the screens and the front pages. Even after this distortion has been allowed for the exceptions to our rule may still appear to be so many and so great as to render it worthless, but they largely disappear upon examination.

In France, Australia and elsewhere parties calling themselves socialist have been voted into office, but these are hybrids like the British Labour Party, in which the large and powerful main body of trade unionists, and others seeking better conditions within capitalism, outweighs the small socialist section. In a number of countries, including the one with the largest population and one of the two super-powers, parties flying one or another version of the Marxist banner have controlled the state. It may seem perverse to say that here, also, communism has been a minority movement, but there are good grounds for doing so. I am using "communism" in the classical sense, to mean a humane, non-militarist, non-nationalist society emerging from revolution, with full political freedom and without class divisions, in which the means of production are owned and democratically controlled by the people as a whole. (Also, by extension, the movement advocating such a society). This is what Karl Marx, founder of the communist movement, meant by the term, but nothing reasonably close to it has appeared in the so-called communist countries. Periods of disorder opened the way for communist parties to grasp control of the state, but the outcome has not matched either the hopes of these groups or the fears of their opponents. Following Marx's prescription the expropriators were expropriated, but most of the workers and peasants refused to play their allotted part.

In Russia the adoption in 1917 of the famous slogan "All Power to the Soviets" (that is, to the democratically-elected governing committees of the time) indicated the belief of the Bolshevik leaders that, the rule of the oppressors having been overthrown, the people would now take over and build the new society for themselves. It did not work out like that. As the dust settled after the upheaval the new leaders found the way forward blocked by a non-communist, non-socialist, non-anarchist majority. Rational persuasion did not win general acceptance for the new ideas, and propaganda had little more effect. The popular demand was for distribution of the land, not collectivisation of it, and the stubborn persistence of the general body of the people in pursuing their private interests proved to be the rock on which the attempt to establish communism came to grief. They showed no enthusiasm for merging themselves into one great economic community but persisted in acting as independent individuals, some operating farms and businesses, others pursuing their private interests as employees. The resistance against collectivisation was strong enough to oblige Lenin to ease the pressure for adoption of the new methods; with the New Economic Policy adopted in 1921 the Bolsheviks accepted a strong element of competition and private ownership into the economy.

In the 1930s under Stalin the attempt at collectivisation was renewed, this time using the full coercive power of the state. It produced one of the greatest man-made famines, but as an attempt to establish communist or socialist principles as a basis for the operation of Russian society it failed; the tendency for individual people and groups to pursue their own economic interests, irrespective of the effect upon the community, could not be eliminated. What took place, under the name of collectivisation, was little more than what has happened, less violently, in the West; the emergence of a small number of large units which swallowed up most of the small ones. The collective farms and great industrial and commercial undertakings of the USSR equate with the agri-businesses, the conglomerates and multinationals, that dominate Western production and distribution. In each country economic activities are motivated by the pursuit of individual satisfactions rather than a regard for the welfare of the community, the main differences being that in Russia the control exercised by government is more open and direct, and the greatest benefits go to high-level bureaucrats as inflated salaries and privileges rather than to capitalists as profits.

In Russia in 1917 the great numbers who constitute the bulk and substance of society, workers and poor peasants as much as bourgeoisie and kulaks, tended to think as a body and to act in economic affairs as individuals, favouring the modes of behaviour Lenin and his colleagues were working against. The Revolution had less to do with any mass movement towards communism than with the inability of Tsarism to cope with the stresses imposed by the First World War. With the great majority seeking a return to accustomed ways of living after 1917 the communist minority, even though now in control of the state machinery, were powerless to bring about the changes they sought. After the revolutionaries and their heirs had been in control in the USSR for nearly three generations communism, and socialism too, remained hardly more than an aspiration, the society continuing to operate its economy rather by competition than co-operation, exhibiting divisions between rich and poor, between those who command and those who obey, as wide as in any professedly capitalist country, and with militarism and nationalism flourishing. The course of events in Russia since the revolution indicates the continuing presence there of political groups corresponding, in their relative sizes, degrees of influence and principal features, to those found in Britain.

Explanations have been offered, for the failure of the Russian Revolution to produce the expected results, ranging from the feeble to the fantastic. Stalin was an Asiatic, Lenin no Marxist but a secret follower of the conspiratist Blanqui, the rulers were in the pay of Western capitalists. They are beside the point, for no leaders, however strong and pure their convictions, could have established communism, or socialism either, in the face of a great majority otherwise inclined.

In China the drive towards communism came in the shape of repeated pushes alternating with periods of relaxation; there, also, the initiative was defeated by the undemonstrative but determined adherence of the people to their accustomed ways. The works of William Hinton, a supporter of the revolution who lived in the country for long periods at the relevant times, provide illumination.

The Maoists claimed that the masses and their hero-leader, driving forward together towards socialism, had been frustrated by entrenched bureaucrats[1]. Hinton loyally tries to persuade himself and the reader to accept this authorised version of events, but reality keeps breaking through. His narrative shows that the repeated drives towards communism – the Socialist Education Movement, the Great Leap Forward, the Cultural Revolution – were not undertaken by Mao together with the masses. It may well be true that Mao provided the initial impulses but each of them, although supported by many activists of the Chinese Communist Party, was passively *resisted* by the broad masses and it was this, rather than any cunning manoeuvres of a minority of bureaucrats, that defeated them. The attempt to induce the general body of the people to work primarily for the collectivity to which they belonged was a failure. At the beginning of the Great Leap the East Wind Commune guaranteed each of its members

---

[1] Hinton 1983, 704

three meals a day and two-and-a-half yuan in wages even if they did no work at all. This was the outcome:

> Since everyone could eat free of charge and everyone who lay at home all day got paid, those who had always been most active began to slow down. If one could eat and earn whether one worked or not, why work[1]?

The interests of the commune did not come into it, let alone those of the wider Chinese community, and the welfare of the workers of the world was still less relevant. What mattered was the individual interests of the people concerned, and an advantageous trade-off of work against rewards ranked high: "While political rhetoric remained militantly socialist, reality tended towards the 'capitalist road...[2]'"

Communism in the classical sense can only function with the willing cooperation of the overwhelming majority, and in no country has this been forthcoming; the general body of the people, educated and uneducated, rich and poor alike, persist in putting their private interests before those of the community and their sheer numbers, together with their untheorised, almost unthinking tenacity, have dragged social practices towards their end of the range. For decades now Russia and China have been moving, in irregular jerks, towards open recognition that their system works to meet the expectations of the great majority rather than those of the communist minority. We have no good reason for expecting the other "communist" states to follow any very different course.

With local and transient exceptions the same great political classes appear in the states called communist as in the professedly capitalist countries. They are found all over the industrialised world, exhibiting everywhere broadly the same principal features and relationships.

Provided we look past superficial appearances to deeper and more enduring characteristics we can take the correspondence farther; wherever these three political classes appear they are subdivided (again, with temporary and localised

---

[1]Hinton 1983, 250
[2]Hinton 1983, 704

exceptions) in much the same way as in Britain. Under a variety of names, sometimes organised as parties, sometimes not, and often enjoying only restricted freedom of expression, the same movements play their parts in the workings of all developed states.

Taking the supporters of existing society first, these subdivide into one movement emphasising the value of authority in political affairs and another pressing for the maximum of political liberty consistent with the security of the state. Where conditions permit these tend to appear as parties, but the absence of a distinct party does not indicate absence of the movement. No distinct liberal party became established in France, although that country was the original home of European liberalism; but the ideas and the movement made themselves felt as "a smear of liberal persuasions across the entire centre of the party spectrum[1]."

In Soviet Russia all parties except the Communist were suppressed soon after the revolution and every attempt made to spread communist ideas, but no amount of persuasion, propaganda or compulsion could ever get the great body of people to take any principled interest in political affairs. Stalin was seen as the father of his people, and when the need to arouse widespread support became urgent the rulers abandoned the welfare of the workers of the world, proclaiming instead the Great Patriotic War. Liberalism, persisting as a feeling that the Communist Party would operate more effectively if it were more democratic (in the old-fashioned, Western sense of that highly elastic term) began to appear more openly after Khrushchev's secret speech to the Twentieth Party Congress (it must be the world's best-publicised secret) and is strengthening under Gorbachev.

Moving farther along the range, the Labour Party is a peculiarly British construction, the schisms, programmes and commitments of the British communist movement find no accurate reflection abroad, and British anarchists have concerns they do not share with those of any other country, But the socialist, communist and anarchist attitudes towards political

---

[1]Bentley 1987, 10

and economic affairs appear in all industrial societies. Indeed, it is misleading to speak of societies in the plural for industrial society now forms one world-wide system, everywhere exhibiting substantially the same structure both political and economic.

The political structure of the civilised world comprises (to use the British names for movements appearing elsewhere under other titles) the non-politicals, conservatism, liberalism, socialism, communism and anarchism, the movements becoming smaller and less influential as they place greater value upon freedom in political affairs and regulation in economic matters, seek wider and deeper changes, and tend more strongly to accept theory as a guide to action. These relationships cause advanced society, under whatever title it appears, to behave like one of the old clown figures, pointed at the top, rounded and weighted at the bottom; it can be tilted in any direction but persists in returning to a position governed by the mass towards its base.

From Politics to Ideology

WE now have before us six movements (strictly, five movements and one group), each of them extending over most of the world although under various names and with adaptations to suit local conditions. In introducing them I have taken the opportunity of showing that they form a series, and we shall find greater significance in this when we come to discuss the origin and development of ideologies. For the time being we concentrate upon the factors which link the members of each of them constituting them a movement and distinguishing that movement from the others.

The members of each of these movements vary among themselves in income, status, personality, ethnicity, nationality, age, sex, diet, geographical location, heredity, physical constitution, accustomed climate, toughness or tenderness of mind, language, education, upbringing, toilet training, relation to the means of production and particular ideas about political matters. They are linked together, constituted a movement and distinguished from the members of other movements, by their common adherence to certain ideas or beliefs, and the ones most clearly distinctive are those highly general ones we have been speaking of.

In our dealings with the physical world we tend to be more impressed by mountains and canyons than by the presence of a continuous solid surface, and something similar happens in politics. Specific policies and concrete proposals tend to be valued above inclinations and tendencies. Yet these persist while policies and proposals come and go, and the ability to endure forms an important part of what we mean when we describe something as real.

On any particular issue a movement may alter its attitude according to the circumstances. The Communist Party of Great Britain at first opposed British participation in the Second World War and later supported it, even demanding that it become more vigorous. After the war several conservative governments accepted the greater part of the existing state ownership of industry, the party going in enthusiastically for privatisation only under Mrs. Thatcher. Looking at the details, even such large "details" as these, the behaviour of the movements seems erratic, but in each case the particular courses chosen were motivated by one enduring inclination. The SPGB, both when opposing British participation and when supporting it, was following a lead given by the USSR believing that thereby it was helping the move towards a society without political restrictions, one in which the means of production would be commonly owned. The Conservative Party was consistently following its practice of holding back from change until confident the outcome would be beneficial; only with Mrs. Thatcher's accession to leadership did it acquire this confidence. In each case the action taken, although a response to the circumstances, was a response guided by the broad ideas and general beliefs, tendencies and inclinations forming the most stable part of the movement's ideology, and political responses are regularly influenced in this way.

This may sound plausible, even self-evident, but on reflection the establishment of a connection between these general beliefs (etc.) and the people who execute the response presents difficulties. Many of those to whom I have been ascribing a preference for a stable or dynamic society, or opinions about the degree of freedom or control desirable in political or economic systems, and the role properly to be played by theory as a guide to action, would look rather blank if asked to say what they thought about these matters; they have been thinking about particular instances rather than overall tendencies. This shows the terms I have been using, such as broad ideas, and general beliefs, to be inappropriate, for it does not make good sense to speak of people being unaware of their own ideas, or not knowing what beliefs they hold.

The way out of the difficulty lies in the concept of *assumption*. We have all undergone the experience of having it pointed out to us that we acted as we did because, without realising it, we had taken something for granted and the "broad ideas" and "general beliefs" forming the main trunks of the different ideologies tend to be accepted, and to produce their effects, in this way. They do sometimes enter conscious reasoning, particularly among the writers and thinkers, but more often they exercise their influence below the level of awareness.

General ideas and beliefs tend to be recognised as assumptions more readily than particular ones, but no rigid distinction can be drawn, ideas and beliefs do not fall into two classes, the members of one taken for granted and those of the other validated by conclusive evidence. Every idea or belief has some evidence in its favour, even if this be only an illusion or an error, and no one of them is ever established beyond all doubt; there remains always the possibility of misunderstanding, of evidence to the contrary overlooked, of error and illusion. All ideas and beliefs include some element of taking-for-granted and this entitles us to treat them all as assumptions, some better supported than others.

Systematic ideology concerns itself mainly with the effects of assumptions upon behaviour, and for this purpose questions of their truth in any absolute sense are largely irrelevant. It is enough for them to produce their effect, that those holding them believe them[1] to be true, and even this is not always needed. The material objects which appear so solid have been shown to consist mainly of empty space, yet even those who have demonstrated this still step forward boldly, expecting the floor to bear their weight. Conservatism and anarchism cannot both be true in an unqualified sense, yet each of them affects the behaviour of its adherents.

We commonly distinguish between, on the one hand, knowledge, ideas, beliefs and other items of mental furniture which are present to awareness and, on the other, assumptions which are not, but this distinction, too, is one of degree. Knowledge often drops below the level of awareness, needing an effort to recall it, while assumptions are not irrevocably hidden; critical examination of behaviour reveals them. In systematic ideology "assumption" is used to cover the whole range, from assumptions remaining unrecognised unless a special effort be made, through the things known but not at the moment being thought of, to the ideas, beliefs and so on standing in the forefront of awareness.

---

[1] ¶(when they do enter awareness)

An assumption may be well supported or not, present to awareness or not, and true or not. As used in systematic ideology the term includes not only things taken more or less completely for granted but also all knowledge, beliefs, opinions, theories, conclusions, principles, ideas, and so on and so on; all items of cognition. It is, of course, still open to us to use the familiar terms – idea, belief, theory and the rest – when we wish to indicate some particular sort of assumption, and I shall often do so.

All our knowledge of assumptions comes from observation of behaviour, our own or that of others. Some types of behaviour provide more information about assumptions than others, the richest source being speech-behaviour. Most of our knowledge of assumptions comes from written or spoken statements. We noted earlier the strong tendency for political beliefs, especially the broader ones, to come in determinate sets. Having now identified these beliefs as assumptions we can say that an ideology is a set of assumptions. (This, of course, is a first approximation, to be clarified and rendered more definite as our work goes on.)

I have been speaking only of the six main political groupings. More specialised movements, such as trade unionism and anti-abortionism, also possess distinct sets of ideas, beliefs and assumptions, distinct ideologies. These, however, concern smaller areas of behaviour than those of which we have been speaking and they do not form a significant series; each of them is a specialised formulation, adapted to a limited range of purposes and circumstances, of some part of the main range, and in order to show the ideological connections between two or more of them we have to trace them back to their roots in these main ones. For these reasons (and for others appearing later) we distinguish the ideologies upon which our attention has been focused, the ones going to form the main sequence, as the "major" ideologies.

In the next chapter we shall go on to look at some of the effects produced by the major ideologies in fields of activity outside party politics, and in doing this it will be convenient to have names for them which do not suggest that ideology has only political importance. Each set of broad assumptions functions to a large extent as a unity, and this endows the behaviour characteristic of each major ideology with a distinctive quality which I propose to call its *ethos*. The *Shorter Oxford Dictionary* defines ethos as "the prevalent tone of sentiment of a people or community," and the people or community in question here are those identified with the assumptions constituting any one of the major ideologies[1].

In distinguishing this behavioural aspect of the major ideologies we also distinguish, by contrast, their cognitive features, the assumptions of which each is constituted becoming its *eidos*. The ethos is more or less directly displayed, while the deeper features of the eidos usually require analysis to reveal them, and this has the effect that ethos rather than eidos supplies the popular stereotypes. The figure of the wild anarchist, for example, derives less from any widespread awareness of anarchism's tendency towards political individualism than from the repudiation of established society inherent in this movement. The major ideologies are highly complex syndromes, but it will be convenient to denote each of them by its *ethos*.

At one end of our series stand the non-politicals, those who vote either not at all or as seems most advantageous at the time. These are adapting their conduct to the circumstances, following the convenient or advantageous course (the advantages in question not being only material ones) without regard to any more remote or long-term considerations. They display the ethos of *Expediency*.

Adjoining this ideology in the series stands the one finding political expression in conservatism, and this movement distinguishes itself from the non-political group by not seizing the advantage of the moment[2] but guiding itself by considerations such as duty, loyalty, patriotism, consistency, moderation, responsibility, respect for superiors and consideration for inferiors. Here we have the ethos of *Principle*.

---

[1]By this use of "ethos" I intend to bring out, in a less "philosophical" way, the feature Walsby expressed by distinguishing between the form and the content of thinking.

[2]¶... the non-political group by ~~not seizing~~ repressing the tendency to seize the advantage of the moment, ~~but~~ instead guiding itself...

Conservatism will often tolerate practices which embody the principles professed only in a general way, as we speak of a course of action being correct in principle, meaning it may be faulty in detail. It tends to cherish methods and institutions proven viable by experience even when their performance is admittedly defective, rather than risk endangering them in a chase after perfection. O'Sullivan, for example, entitles the first chapter of his book (by no means a hostile study) "Conservative Ideology: a Philosophy of Imperfection."

The next term in the series, liberalism represses this flexibility much as conservatism represses expediency. It seeks to specify principles exactly and put them fully into practice. The liberal emphasis being upon getting things exactly right we identify this as the ethos of *Precision*, but this should not be taken to mean that liberalism always attains precisely the ends it sets itself, for manifestly it does not. The term indicates, rather, that liberalism seeks precision. The tendency of this ethos towards even arithmetical accuracy appears in the maxim of the Utilitarians, recognised precursors of modern liberalism, "the greatest good of the greatest number," and William Beveridge spoke of replacing natural law by the rule of the expert[1]. J. A. Hobson spoke in the same spirit when proposing a system of administration by an expert official class trained for the purpose while elected representatives made known the will and desires of the people; "when a rational Democracy is formed laws, like hats, will be made by persons specially trained to make them[2]." With its almost scientifically precise demarcation of function the concept is distinctively a liberal one.

Unlike these three groups the next term in the series, socialism, does not regard existing society as either acceptable or capable of being rendered so. Even if capitalism held to its professed principles in practice, even if it did so precisely, it would still, socialism holds, impose unacceptable conditions upon the majority of people. Socialism proclaims the need for a substantially different system and sets out to achieve it peacefully by an accumulation of minor changes. It exhibits

---

[1]Quoted by Geoffrey Hawthorn, in *TLS* 14 July 1989
[2]Quoted in Bentley 1987, p.85

the ethos of *Reform*. (Here the term carries the sense of re-shaping; its more limited meaning, of putting right parts of the system that are not working as they should, belongs rather to liberalism).

Communism has already been mentioned; it boldly displays the ethos of *Revolution*, and anarchism goes beyond even this, seeing its function as the elimination of authority and coercion; that accomplished the people themselves, acting as people rather than as anarchists, are to establish and maintain an orderly, humane, peaceful and satisfying society. The ethos of anarchism stresses rejection of all that would limit political-intellectual freedom, and does so the more uncompromisingly as it approaches more closely to the purist condition. It is marked by *Repudiation*.

Relations between the ideologies are by no means as free of stress as this schematic presentation, intended only to intro-duce the names we shall be using for them, may suggest. We shall be taking up the dynamics of the system later, but here it can be said that the hostility so prominent between political movements arises largely from the fact that in developing its characteristic feature (principle, precision and so on) each of them represses that displayed by the movement preceding it in the series, and both repression and resistance to it are resented.

As a useful spin-off from the concept of ethos comes a set of jargon-free names for the major ideologies "themselves," distinct from the political movements through which they find expression. When we denote each of them by its ethos the series runs: Expediency, Principle, Precision, Reform, Rev-olution, Repudiation (with one more to be brought forward later) and I shall refer to them from now on by these terms. The names are not intended, of course, to provide complete definitions of the ideologies but rather to serve the purpose names usually serve, acting so as to speak as handles by which they may conveniently be picked up when required[1].

---

[1] An earlier series of names for these six ideologies ran: protostatic, epistatic, parastatic, protodynamic, epidynamic and paradynamic; for some purposes these possess advantages over the ones used here.

It is becoming clear that we have hold of something more substantial than the set of relatively superficial beliefs, ideas and values usually taken to constitute an ideology. Rather than affecting politics, ideology provides its substance and subject-matter. Rather than the major ideologies being adopted in order to further the pursuit of interests, the interests are determined by the ideologies. Even evidence and reasoning depend upon ideology, rather than the reverse, for the ideology of each movement leads it to reject some facts and arguments and methods of thinking while accepting others. The anarchist journals *Freedom* and *Black Flag* seldom report much of the same news as the *Times*, and when different groups do accept the same fact they commonly give it contrasting values. To socialists the introduction of subsidies for families with young children was a step towards equality; to the SPGB it appeared as a refinement of exploitation, making it possible to reduce the wages of workers without children. What liberals believe to be clear thinking appears to conservatism as arid intellectualism and communism claims to possess a distinctive method of thinking, known as dialectical or historical materialism, which overcomes the limitations of formal logic. Even when we recognise that ideology provides the substance of politics this still does not go far enough; political parties and movements are best understood by taking them to be ideological entities, in the sense that a rock is a physical entity and an animal a biological one.

We opened our enquiry with the observation that the main British political movements fall into two groups, conservatism and liberalism together on the one hand (to these we later added the non-politicals) and socialism, communism and anarchism on the other; going on to consider the movements as forming a series we rather lost sight of this. Some features of social behaviour are best understood in terms of the broader classification and it also has its uses in exposition, for the verbal complications which arise when handling six terms often obscure the point at issue. It is sometimes better to rough out an answer to a problem using the two main categories, going on to the finer divisions afterwards.

During the approach to the British general election of 1987 Norman Tebbit described his Labour Party opponents as "firmly united in fraternal hatred of each other's guts," and the remark brings out a significant difference between the two principal political classes. Only the non-politicals are without political divisions, the conservatives having their "wets" and liberalism having split once under Mr. Gladstone, again in the early 1920s between Lloyd George and Asquith, and again in the 1980s between the Liberal Party and the Social Democratic Party. But although these qualifications have to be made, the predominant tendency in each of these movements is towards fusion, conservatism functioning for the most part as a united movement and liberalism coming more or less together again after each split. In the other ideological class the contrary tendency predominates. Socialism from its beginnings has been less a united movement than a number of sects declaring the need of working together but meeting with limited success in their attempts to do so. Bolshevism originated in a split within the Russian Social Democratic Party and itself split soon after the Russian Revolution into Stalinists and Trotskyists, the two going on to spend much of their energy fighting each other and further schisms developing. Anarchism consists of individual people and small groups so independent of each other that the very existence of an anarchist movement sometimes gets called in question.

Divisiveness commonly appears to those affected as a matter for regret, but not always. Derrida, Hobsbawm and other revolutionaries have spoken against the dangers they see in unity and unanimity; they extol the value "not only of autonomy and local identity, but of every kind of disagreement[1]." In politics, as in physics and geology, the appearance of a split indicates a force at work, and Walsby hit off one of the principal differences between the two great ideological classes by entitling the first the *eidostatic* and the second the *eidodynamic*.

This distinction runs through the major social activities and we shall be going on to trace it and some of its effects

---

[1] Treglown 1989

in fields outside party politics. In doing this we shall be following a pattern which appears repeatedly in the history of thought: a system of regularities first recognised in a limited connection turns out later to apply more widely. Geometry as it had been known for some two thousand years was shown by the non-Euclideans to be one part of a more extensive field; Copernicus, Newton and others showed the earth to be subject to the same laws of celestial mechanics as the (other) heavenly bodies, and a series of investigators culminating in Darwin extended the theory of evolution to include humanity. Each extension brought a massive increase in understanding.

Directing our enquiry first towards politics, as the area in which the influence of ideology was originally perceived, we have found that perception to be the first glimpse of something deeper. Beneath the shifting confusions of the party struggle lies a system of ideologies, each of them responsible for distinctive tendencies on the part of its adherents. This system is not visible as it were to the naked eye, its presence is a conclusion drawn from study of observed behaviour; as we take it into account so the broader trends informing daily politics become more readily comprehensible. A comparison may be drawn with the series of chemical elements; outside the laboratory few of these are encountered in their pure form and the whole series not at all, but relating chemical events and phenomena to the series makes it possible to solve problems otherwise intractable.

Communists and anarchists, whatever their class, income or status, tend to be enthused by the prospect of revolution while conservatives and liberals, rich and poor, educated and uneducated, are likely to be horrified and the non-politicals – workers and employers alike – indifferent or apprehensive. Political behaviour, in this instance as in others, cannot be adequately accounted for by reference to the material conditions of life of the people concerned. It would be absurd to dismiss these as irrelevant, but between the stimulation they provide and the political response elicited something intervenes, something powerful enough and sufficiently independent of social circumstance, to cause people living under similar conditions to respond in contrasting ways, and our investigation indicates that something to be the influence of ideology. It remains, of course, to account for ideology but we have more ground to cover before we can tackle that.

Ideology Beyond Politics

PEOPLE engaged in trades, and in professions outside party politics do not normally think of their activities as influenced by ideology, but governments sometimes take a different view. In Russia after 1917, in Germany after 1933, in China after 1948 and elsewhere at other times, the attempt was made to reduce the workings of a complex society into agreement with the assumptions of a single party (not always the same one), and in each case suppression of competing political movements was found to be not enough. If the society was to function as required the practice of religion, science, education, medicine, manufacturing, art, literature, police, commerce, the military, in fact social activities generally, had to be brought into conformity with the ideology of the ruling party. It was largely the endeavour to achieve this condition that earned these states the epithet "totalitarian," and it was here they met some of their worst internal difficulties, for neither peasants nor workers nor most of the professionals could function effectively without using ideas and practices condemned as non-Aryan or counter-revolutionary. Attempts to enforce compliance weakened the economic structure; the outcome was a deathroll comparable with that of a major war and an eventual return towards acceptance of something close to the old methods. In Russia this appeared first as a temporary shift with the New Economic Policy of 1921 and later as Gorbachev's reforms, in China as a relaxation after each drive towards communism. In Germany intervention from outside broke off any course of development the process might have followed.

The indication, that ideology affects these extra-political activities, loses any power to surprise when we consider the conditions governing purposeful action. It requires an object, and whether this be a banana to reach, a solution to find or a social system to establish we never have full information about it in advance. The banana may prove to be a wax model, the problem insoluble and the social system non-viable. We can find out only by reaching for it, trying to work it out, attempting to set it up, and in order to do any of these things we have to assume it to be in some sense real. Ascription of reality to the object aimed at is a necessary condition for purposeful action. Even when, as with a proposed social system, the object is known to be not yet in existence we still, by aiming at it, show ourselves to be assuming it a real possibility. Purposeful activity is, by definition, activity directed towards an end and therefore governed by it, and that end remains always in some respects unknown. Even if it be re-establishment of a previous condition there will have been changes in the circumstances making it impossible to predict, with full detail and complete certainty, what the outcome will be. The desirability and feasibility of the end being aimed at, as well as its reality, are always to some extent assumed.

We have seen the particular assumptions finding expression in the overt activity of each political movement to be derived from a small number of broad general ones, much as the branches, twigs and leaves of a tree derive from the main trunk. This effect is not limited to politics. The assumptions governing purposeful action can be formulated as propositions and every general proposition, whatever the subject, implies an indefinite number of more particular ones; the proposition that bricks are hard solid objects, for example, implies one about each type of brick and each individual brick. The tree-like structure which results, with successively more particular propositions branching off from the more general ones, affects the assumptions which constitute it (e.g. by endowing them with increased stability) as well as being affected by them; it affects, among others, those involved in the selection of an object to aim at[1]. It is because our ideology is as it is that we pursue the ends we do, in non-political matters as in political. Only our non-purposive behaviour, such as reflexes, emotions and physiological changes, is free of determination by an object, and only that is non-ideological.

Going on to pin down these very general remarks we turn first to the theory of physical science. Here Baconian induc-

---

[1] ¶dendrogram

tion, the view that science advances by way of unrestricted accumulation of evidence, laws and principles emerging in some unspecified way from the accumulation, no longer holds the place it once did. Taken strictly it meant that all evidence, on whatever subject, had to be accepted, and of course no science does or ever did accept all evidence indifferently. With increasing recognition of this Bacon's view has been largely discarded; it has come to be generally accepted (among those who think about such things) that science advances by formulating hypotheses and testing them against the results of experiment and observation, the hypothesis deciding which evidence shall be considered relevant. When the question arises as to what governs the formation of these hypotheses only one answer makes sense. They derive from the pre-existing structure of ideas, beliefs, opinions, assumptions and so on, from the ideology, of the investigator.

In the orthodox view ideology appears as a distortion which shrivels under the hard light of science, yet differences between the various approaches to the study of science arise from the assumptions with which they begin, and this is an ideological feature. Euclidean geometry, for example, sets out to elucidate the implications of a few axioms and these, being propositions accepted without demonstration, clearly rank as assumptions. Systematic ideology considers assumptions worthy of study because when they change behaviour changes, and this applies even in this most scientific of sciences, for when geometers start by making assumptions (adopting axioms) other than those of Euclid they come up with non-Euclidean geometries.

In their professional activities scientists are affected not only by axioms, adopted with intent, but also by assumptions which for the most part have been accepted unawares. Those characteristic of each science direct its attention in a particular direction so much so that even when two sciences study what appears to be the same object they credit it with two different sets of properties. Physics does not normally study living creatures but it can do so, predicting the volume of water a given man will displace if submerged and the impact when he falls from a known height. A physiological report will not mention these attributes, dealing instead with the functioning of his internal organs and the difference finds its origin in different starting assumptions. Physics treats the man as (assumes him to be) a material body, something known to occupy a specific volume of space and move in a straight line at constant speed unless affected by outside influences. Physiology, on the other hand, regarding him as (assuming him to be) a complex system, directs its attention towards his internal functioning rather than his interactions, as a solid mass, with the environment. The approach taken by each study results from the assumptions with which it begins, but few practitioners pay much attention to this; here as in other fields the influence of ideology remains for the most part unrecognised by those affected. Science stands as the stronghold of clear-headed rationality; when the influence of ideology shows up within this fortress there can be small reason for surprise at its appearance elsewhere.

In tracing the influence of ideology beyond politics to social affairs generally we shall still not have reached its limits, for much of our personal behaviour is governed in the same way. Every step we take depends upon the assumption that the ground will bear our weight; every time we reach for something we show ourselves to be assuming it to be where it appears to be. We usually remain unaware of having made these assumptions, but without them we would not behave as we do. We shall see later how people and groups come to make these assumptions rather than those; for the moment, the point is that in order to understand why they act as they do we need to study the assumptions made unawares, their tendency to occur in sets, and relations between these sets, as well as the ideas, beliefs and so on which are present to consciousness.

Occupations can be arranged into groups, each of them operating in accordance with a particular set of broad assumptions, and these sets correspond in their main features with the ideologies we found to underlie the main-sequence parties and movements. These form a series running from the non-political to anarchism or, as we can now say, from Expediency to Repudiation. The nearer to the anarchism / Repudiation end of the range a political movement stands the smaller it tends to be and, consequently, the slighter its influence. The same holds good for the occupations, with the result that once the link has been established between an occupation and "its" major ideology we can predict (at least in relative terms) the maximum degree of effect it is capable of producing upon the social structure.

In discussing this, let us begin with science. Its prestige, although not what it used to be, still stands high enough to tempt one into equating it with reliable knowledge; science right, non-science wrong. A little thought does away with any such tendency, for science advances, and every advance shows the view previously held to have been if not wrong then at least not completely right; some of Newton's work is now accepted only with reservations but nobody, so far as I know, has suggested that it was not fully scientific.

To say that science was not concerned with truth would be absurd; its practitioners strive to accumulate evidence and to formulate propositions in agreement with it. But so do historians, and so do many of us in daily life, without claiming to be scientists. Science could hardly have become what it is without using microscopes, telescopes, balances and other more sophisticated devices, and these all have one purpose: they enable the scientist to perceive, and to measure, distinctions invisible to the unaided senses. Einstein's work was not accepted into the corpus of scientific knowledge until it had been confirmed by observation and the crucial distinction between the results predicted by his theories and those derived from Newton's, could only be measured by the finest of instruments. Number has been called the language of science and the typical activity of scientists, especially of those engaged in the "hard" sciences which provide a model for the rest, consists of counting and measuring. These are of course familiar activities in everyday life, but there we seldom use units smaller than millimetres, grams and seconds, often only inches, ounces and minutes, and science works to finer limits. In astronomy margins of error may be measured in lightyears, but even this carries accuracy beyond the abilities of the layman, who can say only that the stars are far away. A major distinguishing feature of science is the effort to achieve accuracy.

In their professional activity scientists are governed in the short term by the more transient and limited constituents of their ideology (the observations and reasoning of which they are actively aware) but, in a wider view, also by its more general features, prominent among them a high valuation of accuracy, and here we have the link being sought. The practice of science shows it to be an expression of the ideology of Precision. This receives confirmation when we recall that Sir Karl Popper finds widespread support among scientists for his view that in order to rank as scientific propositions must be falsifiable; the more precise they become the more readily they satisfy this requirement.

Precision stands near the middle of the range, it is an ideology in which theorising plays a considerable part, and we therefore expect the activities expressing it to exercise a relatively limited effect. This may seem to be contradicted by the prominence of science in modern industrial (or post-industrial) society but the apparent discrepancy, like the political ones encountered earlier, largely disappears on examination. Science produces laws, principles, knowledge, understanding, and although these do exercise an influence upon society it remains limited and largely indirect. The direct and overwhelming[1] influence is exercised rather by technology, and although this now uses results produced by science it does not itself rank as a scientific activity. Technology existed long before science, starting perhaps when the first digging-stick was shaped and certainly as flint-knapping developed. Unlike science, technology is judged less by the degree of precision attained than by the extent to which it enables us to do what we want, and this links it with the ideology of Expediency. In manipulating the material world, as in political affairs, it is the activities expressing this ideology that exercise the greatest influence.

Having arrived at this point, let us follow through the earlier part of the series, glancing at the relative amount of influence exercised by some of the principal activities linked

---

[1] ¶The ~~direct and overwhelming~~ more direct and greater influence...

with the first three of the major ideologies.

In everyday life we approach the physical world without any principled set of guidelines to limit our actions. So far as social factors or other people are able to affect us we take them into account, but within these limits (set by Expediency) we do whatever seems best calculated to satisfy our wants. This usually means taking care to preserve some items (such as clothing) and destroying others (such as pests), but only because this is usually the easiest method[1]; we sometimes reverse ourselves, throwing away out-of-date clothes and keeping a rat as a pet. We replace accustomed foods and hobbies by new ones without[2] feeling any need to justify our actions, and in person-to-person relationships also we follow our inclination from day to day, spending time with this or that person as our feelings, convenience or preference may indicate.

Over the range occupied by purposeful behaviour in our private and personal affairs we act for the most part by the Expedient ideology.

We all eat, drink, sleep and breathe, and by doing these things readily we show ourselves to be assuming that there is no serious danger to be avoided by staying awake, that the food before us is not explosive or the air around poisonous, and so on. These assumptions sometimes turn out to have been false, but we have to take that risk in order to have even a chance of continuing to live. We make them not because they are true (though when the question arises we usually believe them to be so) but because the balance of advantage lies that way.

Unless we have seriously considered the issue we do not think of ourselves as assuming the presence of the physical world. To the uncritical mind this world is simply *there*; we can see it and feel it. But although we may seem to be in direct contact with the world this is not in fact so; if we can be said to experience any event directly it is the physiological changes in our bodily organs, and the existence of the physical

---

[1] ¶... usually the ~~easiest method~~ most pleasant and convenient way of dealing with them...

[2] ¶... without often feeling...

world is an inference drawn from this evidence. An element of choice enters into it. We can, and sometimes do, assume the indications of our senses to be misleading. When thinking at all closely we say the sun does not really rise, even though we have repeatedly seen this happen. We choose to believe that a stick does not bend as it enters clear water, even though our eyes show it doing so.

Children who have suffered pain together with an impression of glowing red usually connect the two thereafter and are well advised to do so, but the assumption of a linkage is not compulsory[1] and, if made, will sometimes prove false; in later life the child will encounter red glows that do not burn and pain that comes without any visual warning. It is less the truth of the assumption "red glows burn" that leads to its acceptance, than the benefits it offers. Anybody with an interest in science knows that apparently solid objects have been shown to consist mainly of emptiness, fundamental particles doubtfully material, "holes in space" and the like, but we still expect a chair to support our weight. All of us, even philosophers working to disprove the existence of matter, manage our daily lives on the assumption that there really is a physical world "out there"; whether it be true or false, anybody who failed or refused to make it is no longer around to argue their case. The assumption is adopted not because it is true, or because we have no alternative, but because we have found this to be the expedient course. Assumptions adopted for this reason form the base of the Expedient ideology; they enable us better to maintain our individual existence, and with it (although this is not the reason for adopting them) the possibility of going on to develop more sophisticated ways of behaving.

The presence of a substantial body of people whose ideology is restricted to the Expedient assumptions, people without interest in anything much except as it affects them or their personal group, hardly needs demonstrating. The Old Testament prophets were already complaining of the way the people ignored divine command, the priests and ministers

---

[1] ¶... linkage is not ~~compulsory~~ inescapable and...

succeeding them continue to elaborate the theme, and in each General Election speakers of every party complain of widespread apathy. This ideology does not exclude consideration for others, since pleasant relations with those around tend to increase one's own comfort. Neither does it exclude charity, even towards distant objects, for the knowledge of having helped to relieve suffering in Africa does something to increase personal well-being in London and New York. It does, however, exclude action guided by impersonal considerations, such as commitment to any set of religious or political principles, or concern for the exploitation of a class or the freedom of a nation.

The Expedient ideology does not bar its adherents from active participation in social activities, even sophisticated ones. By adapting themselves to particular aspects of the social environment they are enabled to run businesses, follow professions, make investments, take part as shareholders, directors, managers or workers in trades, industries, professions and organisations which, taken as wholes, function in accordance with more sophisticated ideologies. They follow, as we say, the letter rather than the spirit.

The term "Expedient" carries more than a hint of disapproval and later we shall see the reason for this; for the moment the point is that, be it right or wrong, admirable or contemptible, this ideology accounts for the greater part of intentional human behaviour and plays a part in all of it, even in complex and sophisticated undertakings; in working out their theories Marx, Newton and Einstein used the most convenient formulations of the results achieved by their predecessors. Every time we do something in a certain way because that seems to be the quickest, pleasantest, cheapest, easiest, most advantageous way, we are acting by the Expedient ideology.

Although many people act wholly by this ideology and (as we shall see in the next chapter) there was a time when everybody did so, it does not now account for all purposeful behaviour. Martyrs have chosen to die by fire rather than recant, and many people regularly follow the course they believe to be right rather than the convenient or advantageous one. They do not abandon Expediency – they cannot, for over large areas of behaviour no other criterion offers – but in affairs they think important they subject it to other considerations, and by doing this they show themselves to have adopted the ideology of Principle.

Expediency finds its function mainly in private life; its appearance in public affairs usually meets with condemnation. The ideology of Principle, on the other hand, appears mainly in public activities, and particularly those going to establish and secure the existence of organised society. Among these may be named production and distribution, education, medicine, police, administration, authoritarian religion, law and the military. Each of these has its hierarchical organisation and its rules which have to be given precedence over the convenience of the individual people concerned. Each of them tends to support authority and accepted wisdom. Each of them, that is to say, exhibits major features of the ideology of Principle, indicating the presence of the total configuration. This does not mean that for the occupation to serve its social function everybody engaged in it has to be committed to this ideology, only that enough of them have to be strongly enough identified with it to ensure that its tendencies predominate.

Teachers are sometimes misleading, police untrustworthy, soldiers cowardly, workers idle and employers rapacious; in every occupation people may be found who follow their own convenience or advantage rather than the accepted principles. Larger numbers offer only external compliance, doing what is required of them because they find that the Expedient course rather than from any commitment to honesty, reliability, punctuality, respect for superiors, consideration for inferiors and so on. But although some, and even many, people within each occupational group may act by Expediency the group cannot perform its social function in this way. Only by adhering to the established practices and standards, even when it is inexpedient to do so, can it maintain the consistency which permits its integration with the other activities going to constitute a functioning society.

Social production and government stand as the distinctive marks of organised society, and they come together. Without them the prevailing tendency continues to be adaptation to the natural environment, while the community that develops them, although still dependent upon the natural world, sets itself to remould that world into conformity with its beliefs, accepting willy-nilly the risks entailed. Principle functions by dominating tendencies towards Expediency; a structure of two levels, the upper dominating the lower, characterises appearances of this ideology, and while this is particularly true of government, social production displays the feature with almost equal clarity. It dominates the raw materials it works with, and although we can easily imagine a condition in which all engaged in production shall stand level with each other, in every society known to history operation of the productive system has entailed the domination of some over others. Every civilised society has developed authoritarian religion and this stresses the value not only of (what religious people regard as) due subjection in worldly affairs but also the need to regulate behaviour in accordance with established standards both moral and intellectual. Expedient people who have been born into a religious community tend to accept the faith unquestioningly without allowing it greatly to affect their actions or their thinking, but with the transition to the ideology of principle this easy outward compliance comes to be replaced by a more serious concern. This is how John Henry (later Cardinal) Newman treated the change in his novel *Loss and Gain*. First, the Expedient condition:

> When, then, men for the first time look upon the world of politics or religion... they have no consistency in their arguments; that is, they argue one way to-day, and not exactly the other way to-morrow, but indirectly the other way, at random. Their lines of argument diverge; nothing comes to a point; there is no one centre in which their mind sits, on which their judgment of men and things proceeds. This is the state of many men all through life; and miserable politicians or Churchmen they make, unless by good luck they are in sage hands, and ruled by

> others, or are pledged to a course. Else they are at the mercy of the winds and waves; and, without being Radical, Whig, Tory or Conservative, High Church or Low Church, they do Whig acts, Tory acts, Catholic acts, and heretical acts, as the fit takes them, or as events or parties drive them.

In the next passage Newman's hero, a likeable, easy-going young student of divinity, is moving towards the religious form of the ideology of Principle, in which systematic thinking begins and responsibility becomes an issue. He finds it:

> more or less antagonistic to his own favourite maxim that it was a duty to be pleased with everyone. Contradictions could not both be real; when an affirmative was true, a negative was false. All doctrines could not be equally sound; there was a right and a wrong. The theory of dogmatic truth as opposed to latitudinarianism (he did not know their names or their history, or suspect what was going on within him) had... gradually begun to energise in his mind[1].

Sir Thomas Browne brings out the satisfaction found by religious people in a submission to established order and routine abhorrent to the reformers and revolutionaries: "Yet at my devotion I love to use the civility of my knee, my hat and my hand[2]." Literature often does illuminate ideology; as an example of Expediency directly facing Principle I offer Falstaff confronted with Prince Hal living up to his new dignity of kingship.

Those who accept a share of responsibility for the establishment and maintenance of the polity (in whatever capacity and on whatever social or economic level) cannot simply extend their former concern with a number of individual people; it is not possible for them to acquaint themselves personally with the millions who make up a modern nation (to speak

---

[1] Newman 1986, 15-16, 27
[2] Cohen 1960

of no greater unit). What they can and do undertake is to subordinate their own advantage and convenience to the practices, rules, traditions, conventions and so on, in a word to the principles, which experience has shown to be effective guides to the maintenance of a viable society.

The undertakings which operate by Principle never quite fulfill their promise. No matter how hard the producers work production does not satisfy demand; the army defeats one enemy only to be challenged by another, education never finally conquers ignorance or religion sin. Medicine does not eliminate illness, or the police crime and disorder, and the state never manages to provide complete security for all citizens. Each of these activities, although successful in principle, leaves something still to be achieved, and the next group of work-activities takes up at this point, seeking to perfect what has been partly accomplished.

This third group embodies the ideology of Precision. It comprises (among other things) formal logic, exact accountancy and non-conformist religion – seeking to correct the defects respectively of principled thinking, of commerce and of worship – but science stands out as its most prestigious member. It is mainly the quantitative precision achieved by physics that has established it as the model science, and this feature even goes far towards transforming into science activities that without it would not deserve the title, Newton's biographer remarking that the accuracy and careful explicitness of his work came close to doing this with alchemy[1].

Unlike religion, education, production and the other activities common to all organised societies, science aims beyond getting things right in principle. The scientists who most fully satisfy the requirements of their profession value themselves by the accuracy of their results and take for granted the consistency, honesty, responsibility and so on whose importance is stressed by the preceding group. Where religion, education, police, medicine and the military find their political equivalent in conservatism, science correlates rather with liberalism, with its concern to establish precise quantitative democracy

---

[1]Westfall 1980, 365-6

and *exact* embodiment of Principle.

Precision in its turn proves unable to overcome all difficulties. The consequences of science are not uniformly desirable, the most careful accountancy provides no guarantee against business failure, and rigorous logic remains largely confined to the classroom and the textbook. The effort to render these activities more effective continues, but another response to their restricted success is the adoption of more radical methods. From this point on the further activities appearing, those expressing the ideologies of Reform, Revolution and Repudiation become increasingly linked with political criticism of society, and since our object here is to show that the influence of ideology is not limited to politics but affects also other social activities enough has perhaps been said to make the point.

In extra-political activities, as in political, some analysis often has to be carried out before the regularity of the relationship, between position in the range and degree of influence exercised, becomes clear. It will probably have been accepted that the occupations embodying the ideology of Precision, whatever their intellectual value, exercise less social influence than those working to establish principles. Non-conformism, logic, accountancy and science function as secondary adjuncts of, respectively, institutional religion, principled thinking, commerce, and the military-industrial complex. To the suggestion that the ideology of Expediency exercises greater influence even than that of principle some resistance has to be expected, for the belief that commerce, industry and government together wield the supreme influence over our society has become one of the unexamined cliches of current thinking. Yet these, and the military too, all operate within limits set by the great body of Expedient people. What these, or the majority of them or, sometimes, even a substantial minority of them, are not willing to tolerate, is thereby excluded from the range of available options. The politicians have a phrase for it: "politically impossible."

Paradoxical as it may sound, consumption came before production, the first people living on what grew naturally, and consumption belongs to Expediency. Action in accordance with the more sophisticated ideologies may facilitate, restrain or modify consumption, but people eat and drink, use transportation, clothing and shelter, not on moral or scientific grounds but because they find it more convenient to do so than not. Production began as a way of enabling a pre-existing tendency to be pursued more effectively and it remains in this secondary position, being able to operate only within the limits of what people are willing to consume. The capitalist cannot continue in business if his goods do not sell and the "creation" of demand is more accurately described as either the recognition of a potential demand hitherto unrecognised[1] or the provision of a new and more effective satisfaction; many successful businesses demonstrate their appreciation of this by the amount they spend on market research. I am not suggesting that humanity came into existence complete with a longing for fitted kitchens and Ferraris, but that greater comfort and increased mobility have always been welcome. Anybody producing a device to make cooking more laborious, or to force the user to remain stationary for long periods, is going to find a more limited market, and the size of their advertising budget won't make much difference. As the Precision-activities serve those of principle so the Principle-activities serve the Expedient.

In addition to all this, Expediency controls the unconsidered part of our intentional behaviour. Every time we do simply what we wish, or what is convenient, without bringing principles to bear or making any effort to achieve precision, we act under the influence of the Expedient ideology. And even when we do follow a principled or precise course of conduct the small items which make it up, the words used and the movements made, are still governed by Expediency, for in these details no other guide appears. The influence of the Expedient ideology upon actions performed incidentally, in the pursuit of some larger object, remains for the most part below the threshold of awareness, but it is no less effective for that. Expediency stands as the most common of all modes of behaviour, being usually what we mean when we describe an

---

[1] ¶... hitherto ~~unrecognised~~ unperceived or...

action as "only natural."

Expediency inclines us towards taking what we want, without offering any value in return. Most people rarely do this, but the presence and strength of the inclination show up in the size, expense and complexity of the social arrangements designed to repress it. Legal systems, police and punishment make up much of the substance of any industrial society and, beyond these, all the vast apparatus of commercial record-keeping finds its chief function in discouraging people from following this tendency. When this is added to what has been said above then, I suggest, we are bound to recognise that neither precision nor principle but Expediency exerts the broadest and deepest influence on our society and accounts for the greater part of its structure.

Expediency undergoes increasing repression as first Principle and then Precision appear (and more yet from the other major ideologies we have still to consider). The forms of its public expression are largely controlled by them, but control is a reciprocal relationship, controllers having to adapt their behaviour to the characteristics of that which they seek to master. The horse imposes requirements upon the rider, and Expediency does the same with Principle and Precision. Just because it is what they dominate and render precise, it controls them as well as them controlling it; in order to achieve their object they are obliged to adapt themselves to its characteristics. Society may well be seen as an organisation for the control of Expediency; an organisation, therefore, whose structure is largely determined by this feature.

An abiding temptation would have us think of an ideology as adapted for performance of an activity, but the phrase suggests that the activity can be performed, if less competently, without recourse to the ideology, when in fact the two are inseparable. The performance of activities (including of course speech-activities) implying that those engaged in them hold the assumptions constituting the ideology provides the sole evidence of its presence. Equally, the performance of such activities indicates the presence of the ideology; performance cannot take place beforehand, the ideology coming along later to help. The activities *are* the ideology, externalised in particular actions; the ideology *is* the activities, internalised as a set of general assumptions[1].

Minor, transient assumptions set our minor, short-term objectives, but these imply the presence of broad, long-term ones. We handle fire cautiously, take care crossing the road, avoid precipices and dangerous animals; in each particular situation our behaviour is immediately governed by particular assumptions concerning this fire or that tiger, but it all falls under the general head of self-preservation and implies the general assumption that it is better to maintain our individual existence than not to do so. Sometimes this assumption changes, one of us coming to assume it better to put an end to life; then behaviour changes in one or more particular connections.

Our next task must be to trace the historical emergence of the ideologies of Expediency, Principle and Precision, and the results of the efforts of their adherents to realise them in social practice.

---

[1] ¶[We can almost say that the] activities *are* the ideology, externalised in particular actions, [and] the ideology *is* the activities, internalised as a set of general assumptions.

The Beginnings

EARLY societies displayed a narrower range of activities than those we know today, showing their ideological structure to have been less complex. Go back two hundred years and our anarchist, communist and socialist movements dwindle to a few scattered visionaries. Another two hundred, to the Sixteenth Century, science and the political outlook we know as liberalism have almost gone. Continuing backwards in time one function after another vanishes until even government, farming and herding have disappeared. The first people knew nothing of money, monarchs, armies, agriculture, priests, employment, unemployment or taxes.

Homo sapiens sapiens came on the scene some forty thousand years ago and sapiens about a quarter-million years before that, while accepting *Homo erectus* as human can take the origins of humanity back three or even four million years[1]. Agriculture and government, on the other hand, are only about ten thousand years old. Food-production and administration constitute the essence of what we mean by a society, but for much the greater part of the time since humanity first appeared everybody lived in communities without either of them, and some continued to do so down to modern times. These included the Polar Eskimo, the Australian Aborigines, the Kalahari Bushmen, pygmies living in the Ituri forest of Central Africa, peoples of India, Malaysia, South America and elsewhere, but not many of them, perhaps none at all, are still keeping closely to the original way of life. The Eskimo use guns, snow-mobiles and outboard motors, the Australian Aborigines fight for their land in the law-courts, many of the Kalahari Bushmen are only part-time foragers, living mainly from their employment by the neighbouring Bantu farmers, and in a photograph of an Ituri encampment one pygmy occupies a folding chair, neatly making the point that every community directly studied has been affected by contact with civilisation[2]. Fortunately they retained their distinctive characteristics long enough for these to be recorded, and it is from

---

[1] Flood 1983, 30
[2] Turnbull 1984, plate 4

study of these communities, as well as of the archaeological record, that our knowledge of the way of life of the earliest people is derived.

The peoples directly studied cannot safely be assumed to have been in their original condition. They stand as far in time from the origin of humanity as ourselves and none have remained in isolation; Australia for example, was being visited from Indonesia long before Captain Cook arrived. Direct knowledge of the earliest way of life in its purity is not to be had, but if we accept that human beings evolved out of the animal kingdom then we have to take it that during the long ages from which only a few scattered bones and shaped stones have come down to us they were moving from the condition of humanoids, difficult to distinguish from animals, towards that of the simplest communities known.

The evidence indicates that they lived in small bands, rarely of much over fifty people, but occupying – or at least ranging over – surprisingly large areas. In the American Great Basin the density of population (if "density" be the word) ran at about one person to fifteen square miles and, in the central desert, one to forty square miles[1]. Each band would be in contact with others, its members aware of themselves as members of a tribe and even of a people, and numbers of bands might congregate on occasion, but neither the band nor any larger assembly constituted anything comparable to a state. There was no overriding authority, the structure being of the type known to social anthropologists as segmental, its constituent parts – mainly kinship-groups – standing beside rather than above one another.

Organised very differently from our own societies, they also behaved in a different way towards their natural environment, directly consuming what it provided rather than treating it as a source of raw materials to be adapted to their own requirements. We cannot say that they did not engage in production, for many made digging-sticks (though more for collection than cultivation), and Australian Aborigines were operating a flint-quarry centuries before the Europeans

---

[1]Service 1966, 94

arrived. The fishing tribes of the Northwest Coast of North America built large timber houses with elaborate ornamentation, and made enough besides to indulge in the competitions of destruction known as potlatches. All the collecting peoples to survive into modern times wore some sort of clothing and constructed shelters if not always dwellings, the Eskimo in particular being renowned for the refined technology displayed in their tools, clothes and igloos. One writer suggests that people living without government produced the first cities, agriculture being less a cause than a consequence of these[1], and the landscape, in prehistoric Australia and parts of the American Great Basin, was to some extent an artifact, produced by repeatedly burning off the undergrowth (though this may not have been intentional)[2].

Members of the early communities produced a great deal but for the most part as individuals meeting their individual needs; they did not depend upon social systems of production. Above all they did not grow their own food[3]. Some of them may have done some irrigation to promote natural growth, or scratched the soil to produce supplements to their diet such as tobacco or onions, but they did not produce the staples on which they relied.

Here we pause for a moment to clarify the way in which "production" is being used. In one sense of the word a hunter can be said to produce meat, but in that sense every action upon the material world produces something, treading on a piece of chalk produces powder and even the most straightforward consumption is also productive – of worn-out clothes and masticated food. The word loses specific meaning, becoming almost a synonym for "action." There is another sense in which production is distinguished from consumption, a sense in which hunting and gathering is not productive but a part of consumption, belonging to the same category of behaviour as lifting food to the mouth. In this more specific sense food-production began with agriculture, and in this sense the term

---

[1] Jacobs 1970, passim

[2] Flood 1983, 237, 201, 205, 213

[3] ¶... systems of production. ~~Above all~~ , and above all, they did not grow their own food. ~~Some of them may have done some~~ Many of them carried out irrigation...

is used here. But to return to our main theme.

These early people gathered the fruits, grains, roots, herbs and nuts which grew naturally, and hunted animals but did not domesticate them. (Not even the dog; the earliest known skeleton of a domesticated dog, at Star Carr, dates from around 8,000 B.C., when agriculture was beginning).

When people living in this way first came to the attention of scholars they were known as hunters but later as hunter-gatherers[1], for with a few exceptions such as the Eskimo they lived more on the roots, nuts, and so forth collected by the women than on the animals hunted by the men. More recently they have increasingly come to be called foragers or collectors. For our purposes these newer terms also carry disadvantages and I shall use "the early people," "the original way of life," or some equally vague equivalent until our enquiry turns up a more descriptive title.

Among the first anthropologists to make a serious study of any of the peoples living in this way was Lewis Henry Morgan, whose results were used by Friedrich Engels in his book, *The Origin of the Family, Private Property and the State*. Since 1884, when this first appeared, the people known to Marxists as hunter-gatherers have occupied a special place in communist theory[2] as having enjoyed "primitive communism," thus providing a model, though a restricted one, of the society this movement seeks to establish. Some modern anthropologists support this view[3] but others reject it, sometimes vigorously. One condemns it as "superficial" and "misleading[4]" and another as "Victorian pseudo-anthropology[5]." Morgan based broad generalisations on studies of the Iroquois, and since Engels wrote increasing knowledge has shown that some of these cannot be maintained, for other peoples behave differently. This revision has been established well enough for at least one organisation claiming to be Marxist to have admit-

---

[1] ¶ ~~The term is Although an advance~~ first to hunter and then hunter-gatherer, although an advance, even the second term hardly seems to go far enough

[2] ¶ Since 1884, when this first appeared, the ~~people known to Marxists as~~ hunter-gatherers have occupied a special place in ~~communist~~ Marxist theory...

[3] Leacock and Lee 1982, Introduction

[4] Service 1966, 17, 24

[5] Clark 1983, p.63

ted that Engels' book "does not stand up to anthropological scrutiny[1]."

For members of these communities accumulation of possessions was not an object; they owned little more than nomads without domesticated animals could carry, the possessions of a !Kung San of the Kalahari, for example, weighing twenty-five pounds or less. All members of the community enjoyed open access to the territory from which they drew supplies, they were sometimes under an obligation to share their food, and they did not derive power over other people from what they did possess. This does not mean, however, that they followed practices at all close to those advocated by the founders of communism. When several Eskimo joined in pursuit of walrus, the kill did not become the common property of the hunters, let alone of the community, but was divided into individual portions, the hunters' shares being decided by the order in which their spears had entered the animal. Trees bearing favourite fruits were sometimes privately owned by particular families, communities often tried to exclude outsiders from their territory, and the obligation to share did not extend to all comers, or all in need, or even all members of the community, but was commonly restricted to those from whom reciprocation, either "general" or "balanced," could be expected.

The nature of their system of ownership begins to appear when we stop thinking of these communities in static isolation and locate them in the developmental sequence. They stood between the animal world, in which ownership (as distinct from physical possession) is hardly an issue, and societies in which ownership was a major preoccupation, people being valued, and even coming to value themselves, according to the amount they owned. They stood between an earlier condition in which nothing was privately owned and a later one in which almost everything was; what they had is best regarded not as any form of communism but rather as undeveloped private ownership.

---

[1]Socialist Party of Great Britain 1986, 14

These peoples could call upon neither law-courts nor police. Anybody claiming anything had to maintain the claim for themselves with little support from the community, for ownership, a legalistic conception, had hardly begun to emerge from the *de facto* relationship of possession. In economic matters their system (or non-system) was almost wholly individualistic, not more but *less* collectivistic than those that were to follow.

Similarly with such production as they can be said to have undertaken. They hardly used division of labour except as it was forced upon them by differences of age and sex. Instead of relying upon systems of production, and undertaking the co-operation needed if these were to work, they acted for the most part independently, each making for him- or herself what each required. In obtaining what they needed or wanted they acted, to a greater extent than the members of any later society, as independent individuals.

They are sometimes said to have lived in harmony with their environment, but we have no reason to think they practised intentional self-restraint. Unlike the supporters of our ecological movements they were not behaving with thoughtful consideration for the natural world; they used it as their own purposes required and if they committed no irreparable harm this was because they had not the power to do so. One study of the cave paintings, incised tools and rubbish heaps of two Upper Paleolithic sites led to the conclusion that over-hunting of the large game animals had reduced their numbers to an extent that forced reliance upon the more troublesome small game and shellfish[1]. Instead of behaving towards the environment, in the activities which were later to develop into economic systems, as if it and they belonged to the one collectivity, they rather treated it as something they were not obliged to care about, an individual entity separate from themselves.

In one sense these peoples were primitive; they stood at the beginning. If tempted to look down on them, however, we need to remember that they established the first human

---

[1]Mithen 1988

communities, introduced the use of fire, made and used tools in ways the animals do not, and invented language; these may well have been the greatest of human achievements. They deserve our respect for their own accomplishments, they do not need us to ascribe to them systems, or even aspirations, which were to appear only much later. Their economic life was strongly individualistic, and to picture it as predominantly co-operative, let alone communistic, is to render the course of social development incomprehensible. I emphasise that individualism flourished in their *economic* life; their political activities followed a different course.

Looking only at their economic life makes it difficult to see why they formed communities instead of living permanently as separate individuals or nuclear families. The purpose can hardly have been mutual assistance in obtaining supplies, for increasing population in a given area would usually have made it *harder* to find sufficient food; they often dispersed for a large part of the year for this reason. Gathering together was a luxury they indulged in as far as supplies permitted; in their political life they exhibited a tendency the reverse of that shown in economic affairs, not individualistic but collectivistic.

It sounds odd to speak of political life among these people, for the term suggests intellectual conflict, debates, theoretical arguments and struggles for power, and these had not yet appeared. These things all presuppose, however, the presence of a unity solid enough to persist in spite of their divisive effects. The fundamental political act was the establishment of a community, and this the early people accomplished. Their communities, in fact, were so well established, the "cake of custom" (to use Bagehot's phrase) so solid, as hardly to permit the appearance of political or intellectual individuality.

We who live under the restrictions imposed by civilisation tend to think of their absence as freedom, forgetting other limitations. Rousseau's dream of the noble savage, and Hobbes' nightmare of primitive life as a war of every one against every one, both take for granted absence of social control over the individual person, and this assumption rests on inadequate information; membership of an early community entailed restrictions, upon behaviour towards one's fellows, closer than those found in any of the societies that were to develop later. Elman R. Service for example emphasises the power of the social control that operates in small face-to-face societies, speaking of the extreme sensitivity of these people to the feelings of their group. Overt institutions of government are not to be found, but etiquette, custom and socio-psychological sanctions exert even closer control over the behaviour of individual people. In the absence of personal rulers "custom is king[1]."

All communities, both these relatively simple ones and the more complex ones known as societies, require compliance with certain norms and use sanctions to enforce their demands; without this they would be mere aggregations. In the early communities these standards were seldom or never overtly formulated, and this produces a misleading impression of their absence. Remaining almost entirely implicit as habits, expectations, customs and etiquette, transmitted to the young within the family and by elders to their juniors, rather than in any more public or formal way, they were none the less effective for that. No distinct apparatus, no inspectorate or police force, ensured compliance; instead, the community as a whole performed the task. When the inevitable disagreements arose, requiring a community decision, the early folk held to their non-hierarchical methods, seeking unanimity of opinion rather than accepting the continuing presence of a dissenting minority (not that they would have thought in any such terms), and often using a more or less ritualised contest or duel (among the Eskimo a song-duel) to decide which way the decision should go. Sanctions such as gossip, ridicule and withdrawal usually proved effective against deviants, but as a last resort anybody who persisted in actions that could not be tolerated was likely to be killed, with at least the tacit agreement of the community and usually by close relatives, since that was less likely to start a feud. Among some of the peoples of the Northwest Coast of North America, for example, "witches accused of practising black magic were

---

[1] Service 1975, 83

often slain and these killings went unavenged[1]."

This tendency to act, in political-intellectual affairs, as a community rather than as separate individuals Walsby terms "political collectivism." It contrasts with the individualism which these people exhibit in the material-economic field, and when unrestrained it inhibits not only the development of political or intellectual individuality but also the appearance of institutionalised leadership; people threatening to set themselves up as leaders exercising authority get suppressed like other deviants. In his survey of recent anthropological work on the early communities Service says they functioned by influence rather than authority, valued humility, and did not tolerate "bossiness." (He calls them egalitarian but the term carries an unjustified suggestion of set intent on their part; "non-hierarchical," although clumsier, seems more appropriate). They might have leaders or headmen, but not in the sense of command usually associated with the word "chief"; rather as advisers, co-ordinators, directors or initiators of particular undertakings. These were also likely to be the ones expressing the opinion of the band, such "authority" as they possessed being limited to voicing approval of decisions made by the group as a whole. They had to remain sensitive to the opinions and feelings of other members of the band, falling in with their preferences where they could not get their own accepted by persuasion[2].

The nearest the first communities came to possessing an institution of government was what some investigators have called a council of elders; this appeared, for example, among the Aborigines, but without making the claim to a monopoly of force which characterises the state. Harold Barclay describes the aboriginal community as a gerontocracy, adding that the elders resemble grandfathers rather than governors or policemen[3].

The absence of governmental institutions leads some investigators to regard these communities as early examples of anarchism, but the view carries consequences its supporters

---

[1]Barclay 1982, 49
[2]Service 1966, 83
[3]Barclay 1982, 15

seem not to have considered. The period when everybody lived by foraging was succeeded by the world-wide spread of the state, and unless we are going to say this was sent by God, or brought by little green men from Mars, Venus or wherever, we have to accept that it developed out of the first communities. If these were anarchist then it follows that anarchism produced the state.

In these early communities the distinctions between people, and between a person and the group, were not formalised as specific rights and obligations, and this indefiniteness appears also in other fields. Discriminating sharply between the various species of plants which they used, these people tended to lump all others together as of no interest, and although every community studied had at least some apprehension of a supernatural world, none made any clear distinction between the sacred and the secular. In describing Murngin tribal initiation ceremonies Talcott Parsons stresses that the adult man actually becomes a part of the totem, and this does not show that the sacred world has been brought down to the everyday level but that *"the status of sacred objects and secular social unit have not been differentiated*[1]*."* A principal object of initiation ceremonies was to ensure cultural uniformity; in political-intellectual activities the early people sought fusion rather than fission, and to such an extent that they sometimes deified the collectivity. Robert Lowie, in his history of ethnological theory, summarises Durkheim as saying that primitive man was overshadowed by the power and strength of his community, feeling himself a nobody apart from it. Totems were symbols of the clans, and essentially the social unit was God[2]. Not all ethnologists accept Durkheim's identification of God with the society, but few who have studied these early people disagree with him on the political-intellectual identification of the individuals with their community.

It is feasible to dance and sing by oneself but the early people came together to do so. It is practical, at least when supplies are plentiful, to hold supplies of food communally, but they tended to do so separately, their obligation to other

---

[1]Parsons 1977, 35, 36. Emphasis in the original.
[2]Lowie 1937, 205

members of the community being limited to sharing with those from whom gifts could be expected in return. Any impression of this separateness where material goods were concerned only applied when things were easy, that in time of scarcity these people would help each other with supplies, will hardly survive a reading of Turnbull's *Mountain People*, a heartrending account of the behaviour of the Ik to each other and to their children after the inclusion of their hunting-grounds in a game-reserve had brought them to the point of starvation. Each of these communities can be described as a political-intellectual collectivity, without established hierarchy, formed by people who act as independent individuals in economic-material life.

When one thinks at all closely about individualism and collectivism the relationship between them turns out more subtle than at first appears. They are contraries, existing in relation to each other, and any attempt to grasp one of them in isolation finds it turning in the hand. A collectivity consists of individuals, and if this be left out of account it comes back as it were from behind; the pure collectivity cannot be conceived of except against some background, from which it is distinguished as one individual from another. Conversely, any attempt to arrive at pure individuality, stripping away everything the concrete individual has in common with others, leads towards an individual possessing no features, one which cannot be distinguished from any other and disappears into the collectivity. As abstract principles collectivism and individualism are inextricably interwoven, but our concern lies with the behaviour of concrete societies; here they appear as distinct tendencies, and the distinction has a firm base in that human beings are both material-biological and intellectual-social creatures. They inhabit separate bodies; food, and in most parts of the world clothing and shelter too, must be appropriated to the maintenance of each individual one of them. Intellectual life, on the other hand, cannot be more than partly individualised; to pass on an idea is not to deprive oneself of it, and conceptual thinking entails the use of language, a means of communication created by a community[1];

---

[1] ¶See Sapir

the individualistic tendencies that appear in later thinking stand on this base. In displaying economic individualism and political collectivism the early communities are complying with the circumstances in which they find themselves, they are "doing what comes naturally."

The peoples, ancient and modern, who followed this way of life lived, for the most part, from hand to mouth. Where supplies were seasonal they maintained the necessary reserves, but wherever they could survive while following immediate impulse they tended to do so. The Polar Eskimo, inhabiting one of the harshest environments on earth, have been repeatedly described as light-hearted and improvident, happily gorging to the last lump of blubber and leaving tomorrow to look after itself[1], and similar accounts are given of the !Kung and Gikwe Bushmen, living under widely differing conditions at the other end of the earth[2]. They were not purposely enjoying themselves while they could because life is short but doing what comes easiest and following the impulse of the moment. In exhibiting economic individualism and political collectivism they were not moved by any acquaintance with these ponderous polysyllables but following the course of least resistance, and this tendency runs through their life. They did not submit to the self-discipline required for growing their own food but followed the game and the seasons, did not live consistently as either united communities or as separate famines, but followed the practice they found most appropriate to their circumstances of the moment.

The members of these communities valued humility and compliance, neither seeking to impose any personal ideas about the right way to operate a society nor supporting any who might attempt to do so. They did not strive to alter their environment, natural or social, to suit themselves, preferring to adapt their own behaviour to the requirements it imposed. In both the main areas of social activity, the economic-material and the political-intellectual, they chose the immediately convenient route rather than the one offering greater long-term rewards in return for greater effort.

---

[1]Burnford 1974, 103 also Freuchen 1962, 189
[2]Service 1966, 13

When civilised travellers meet people living in this way the encounter commonly produces complaints of their dishonesty and unreliability. Jonathan Benthall quotes extracts from the diaries of three missionaries to the Yupik people of Alaska between 1891 and 1920; they charge the Yupik with being "disgusting, evil-ridden, frivolous, profligate, immoral and unclean[1]" Such complaints come of judging one society by the standards of another. These people themselves place no great value on principles, and the tenor of their life runs against making any effort to follow a predetermined course. It is not they but the student who seeks to unify their behaviour and reduce it to a formula. If they can be said to display a consistent overall tendency at all it lies towards doing the immediately convenient thing, towards expediency. They live in accordance with this ideology, and accordingly our term for them will be the *Expedient* communities, or communities of *Expediency.*

These people are generally known, among those who bother with such issues at all as hunter-gatherers, foragers or collectors, and all these terms accord primacy to economic life; this has become one of the unexamined clichés of current thinking. Bertold Brecht puts it sharply when saying that grub comes before ethics[2]. The assumption has powerful intuitive appeal but observation and enquiry do not support it. Thoughts, beliefs and ethics are already involved in human eating, there seems to be no society or community which does not impose restrictions upon what may properly be consumed. The Eskimo of the Hudson's Bay area had a taboo against eating seal and caribou on the same day[3], one Australian tribe refused to eat a green caterpillar enjoyed by their neighbours[4], and some tribes have sought opportunities to engage in cannibalism while other people have starved to death because they believed it to be wrong. Human beings, whether individually or in groups, do not put thinking aside when they come to satisfy their material needs. There is no purely economic activity,

---

[1] *Anthropology Today* Vol. 5 No. 5, October 1989
[2] Auden & Kronenberger 1964, 368
[3] Boas 1911, 222
[4] Hilliard 1968, 41, quoting an observation by Basedow in 1903.

untouched by thinking, to serve as fundamental determinant of a political-intellectual superstructure.

Political condition and mode of obtaining sustenance are undeniably connected; food-producing societies regularly have institutionalised government with coercive force at its disposal while those which live by collecting are consistently without it. But this does not show the political to be a superstructure based on, and fundamentally determined by, the economic. To live by hunting and gathering precludes the establishment of government but, equally, absence of the organised force that accompanies settled government precludes the constant protection of crops and herds that makes dependence upon food-production feasible. The economic and the political are two parts of a whole, and examination of either reveals the influence of the other; if we are to speak in metaphor they are related not as base and superstructure but rather as two sides of a coin. They can of course be conceptually separated for purposes of study, but the act produces artificial abstractions incapable of independent existence, and if this be forgotten confusion results.

The Expedient communities are well worth studying on their own account, but for our enquiry they have a specific importance. Their conduct expresses their assumptions about the way life ought to be lived, and those assumptions have not disappeared; their continuing influence is implied by the behaviour of immense numbers of people today, even in the great cities. These take little interest in the activities of society at large, having their attention mainly confined to the small group, seldom much larger than the hunter-gatherer band of up to about fifty people, with whom they interact as persons. They show little mental independence, accepting the standards of the society into which they happen to have been born and joining in conversations mainly directed to demonstrating the absence of significant intellectual distinctions between the speakers. But they live in separate homes, have separate incomes, and use separate cars when they can. Today as in palaeolithic times, and in London, New York and Moscow as in Central Australia, the polar regions and the Kalahari, the prevailing tendency in political-intellectual life is collectivistic and in economic-material affairs individualistic. The ideology of Expediency, in which these tendencies appear most strongly, is neither obsolete nor becoming so. Political collectivism provides cohesion, enabling society to contain the stresses resulting from developing technology, and economic individualism provides the motive force driving sophisticated productive and distributive systems. The evidence does not indicate that these tendencies, exhibited by the earliest human communities, are likely to disappear in the course of future transformations.

Hobbes made his sour comments[1] before much was known of the Expedient communities. Reports from anthropologists living among them show that they often enjoyed lives which many of our own people might well envy, with leisure, ample food, an active social life, music, dancing, ritual and the graphic arts; the investigators often regret having to return to civilisation. The persistence of this ideology does not condemn those holding it to lives of nastiness and brutality.

Through long ages everybody lived the Expedient life, but this does not mean that ideological processes remained static. Each major ideology offers unlimited scope for extension of knowledge and for variation in particular ideas, and the Expedient period covers the immense stretch from the first humanoids to communities with elaborate ritual, complicated kinship systems, complex language and the use of fire. But all these advances took place within limitations imposed by the absence of any substantial attempt to alter the main conditions imposed by either the community or the natural environment. About ten thousand years ago, however, things began to change. Political collectivism and economic individualism began to weaken and their contraries to strengthen, the headless Expedient communities to be replaced by structured societies producing their own food. The ideology of Expediency began to be repressed (though not eliminated) by that of Principle.

---

[1]See p. 87

From Village to Empire

SOME ten thousand years ago Expediency, and the communities relying upon it, began to go down before an ideology and a way of life formerly unknown. The new methods, even in their earlier stages, permitted the formation of units up to a thousand times bigger than the previous ones and the changes, taken together, constitute the transition from community to society.

Among the most prominent features of the development was a shift from foraging to reliance upon cultivated foods. Gordon Childe christened this change the Neolithic Revolution[1] but it extended over some two thousand years and, in some locations at least, took even longer; in the Tehuacan Valley cultivation began around 7200 B.C., but not until almost five thousand years later did agricultural products come to make up seventy per cent of the diet[2]. Only the fact that the preceding Palaeolithic had lasted at least two hundred thousand years enabled such a leisurely transition to rank as a revolution.

The introduction of agriculture, and the changes in diet which it brought, have sometimes left physical traces, but the social structures which originally accompanied them have vanished. We have to infer the characteristics of these, mainly from observation of ways of life surviving into modern times, and the indications are that in social structures of the new type the inconsequence, segmental structure and person-to-person relationships of the Expedient community came to be overridden by recognised obligations, hierarchical organisation and relations between groups distinguished by occupation and status. The transition once achieved, the society did not have far to go before the new features consolidated into a state and a system of government.

Our study began with a survey of the range of political movements, and in order to bring the whole of this into view we had to stand back far enough to lose sight of many

---

[1] Childe 1936, 80
[2] Service 1975, 16

details. Selection of an appropriate scale is a condition of useful enquiry, the map showing each field and building will not display the outline of the country, and close study of individual societies would not help us to establish any clear distinction between Expediency and its successor. We shall not plunge into the complexities which arise when seeking to specify exactly the differences between a headman, a bigman and a chief, or the regularity with which a particular form of social organisation accompanies one or another type of horticulture. We shall not need even to take account of the difference between horticulture (using the hoe) and true agriculture (with the plough), distinguishing only between societies which produce the food on which they depend and exhibit institutions of government on the one hand, and communities which do neither of these things on the other. I shall bring forward one society close to the borderline in order to show that even here changes in the way the means of life are obtained accompany major changes in the political-intellectual structure, but it is in the flower rather than the seed that distinctive features appear in full and accordingly our main attention will focus upon kingdoms and above.

In his classic study of the Nuer of the Southern Sudan Evans-Pritchard presents them as naked cattle-herders, seasonally nomadic[1], living in grass huts and supplementing their diet of animal products by horticulture. They form a congeries of tribes, sometimes gathering into loose federations but without central administration, rulers or grading of warriors or elders, and the age-sets into which they are divided have no corporate function. Evans-Pritchard speaks of "leopard-skin chiefs" among them, but makes it clear that this position is backed by no coercive force. They show some specialisation but nothing amounting to a profession and cannot be said in any strict sense to have law, for there is no authority with power to adjudicate or enforce a verdict. In sum, "their state might be described as an ordered anarchy[2]."

When these people are compared with those of developed states their way of living seems primitive; only when we set

---

[1] ¶(transhumant)
[2] Evans-Pritchard 1950, 5,7,90,110,134,180

them against the Expedient communities does the full force of other observations in the same book become clear. The leopard-skin chief is a sacred person with a specialised function, and blood must not be shed in his presence. The Nuer pride themselves upon their cattle (sometimes obtained in war), fighting among themselves over them and using them to buy brides; their herding cannot be accomplished by families acting independently but requires an extensive tribal organisation using recognised conventions in the settlement of disputes. Small local groups tend to act together, forming "economic corporations" and a political system involving "structural relations between territorial segments larger than village communities." War with the neighbouring Dinka "may be called an established institution." Within each tribe blood-wealth is paid in compensation for homicide, meaning that there is a limited form of law within though not between the tribes. One clan is sometimes dominant in one or more tribal areas and the Nuer occupy a dominant position among their neighbours. Ceremonial sacrifice of sheep and oxen is regular practice, and the life requires the shepherd virtues of courage, love of fighting and contempt for hunger and hardship. Regarding herding as their proper occupation they yet accept the necessity for the hard, unpleasant labour of horticulture.

Each of these features distinguishes this society from the peoples who live Expediently, and the point gets driven solidly home when we read that among the Nuer: "The feud is a political institution being an approved and regulated mode of behaviour between communities within a tribe"; bound by custom as each of the expedient communities may be, approved and regulated modes of behaviour play little part in relations between them. Finally, and for our purposes conclusively, Evans-Pritchard credits the Nuer with a state, a headless kinship state which maintains order and establishes social relations over wide areas; when he describes them as living in an ordered anarchy the "ordered" is not to be overlooked[1].

---

[1] Evans-Pritchard 1950, 5-181

In order to maintain their way of life the Nuer have to give the needs of the cattle priority over their own convenience and, what they find more onerous, to undertake also the labour of horticulture. They have to respect the property of their fellows in the owner's absence, and the need to work together in caring for the herds means that each of them has to submit to established methods of resolving disputes.

Those who would depend upon farming need to preserve cattle and crops whatever the stress, giving prudence, foresightedness, thrift and industry priority over immediate convenience. Famine has occurred repeatedly over much of the world throughout history, and Expediency requires that in hungry times all available food be eaten, but if this be extended to the seed-corn and the breeding cattle then the people revert to living on what they can collect. The transition from foraging to dependence upon herding, horticulture or farming cannot be accomplished without the imposition of severe restraint upon the tendency to do what is immediately convenient; it requires acceptance of the assumption that unrestrained Expediency is insufficient. As the approved criterion, of those parts of behaviour which affect public affairs, Expediency comes to be subordinated to Principle.

Expediency cannot be eliminated, for in much of personal life no other criterion can operate, and the same holds for the small actions making up the extended courses of behaviour to which principles do apply. The herdsman is obliged to go and look after the cattle and the housewife to cook the food, but they decide for themselves which foot to step off with, which hand to hold the pot in. These decisions are governed by Expediency alone, but unless they be made the new system cannot function. Where the hunter-gatherer communities exhibited only Expediency, their successor displays both Expediency and Principle, but these two do not stand passively side by side. In order to function Principle has to repress Expediency and this pattern of two levels, one dominating the other, characterises the many features which distinguish the new society from the old community.

Unlike the foraging communities, food-producing societies display stratification, all but the simplest of them possessing institutions of government with coercive force at their disposal. Also – again unlike the expedient communities – they seek to control their environment, deciding how and where their crops and herds shall grow and requiring their members to perform the tasks entailed, from ruling to mucking out, whether it suits them to do so or not. Expediency gets pushed into the background, hierarchical organisation comes to predominate over segments and the community of Expediency becomes the society of Domination.

The change entails the emergence of distinct occupational groups, usually in complementary pairs and almost invariably with one member of each pair dominating the other. Food-producing societies beyond the very simplest live under permanent chiefs – a different thing from the informal and personal influence, with occasional resort to temporary leaders, found among the expedient peoples – and as the societies develop monarchs come to dominate their subjects, employers their workers, masters their servants, teachers their pupils, preachers their congregations and officers their soldiers, specialisations unknown to the expedient communities. Among the people who live by collecting, and even among animals, one may dominate others (Goodall, writing on chimpanzees, indexes twelve entries under "hierarchy")[1] but there the supremacy depends upon the personal qualities of the individuals in question, while as the societies of Domination develop social status comes to be largely divorced from ability, rulers often being inferior, in mentality, physique and charisma, to many of their subjects. The feature in question is not, strictly, domination, it is the institutionalisation of domination, but this being an impossible phrase to use repeatedly I shall continue to use mostly the shorter form, relying on the context to supply the rest.

When kings replace chieftains as supreme rulers, and sometimes even before that, the few who own much begin to stand out from the many who own little, and the distance between them increases with further development. It makes the economic behaviour found in these systems seem more

---

[1]Lawick-Goodall 1974, Index

individualistic than what has gone before, but closer examination dispels this appearance. In the Expedient communities what little production took place was almost always for the direct benefit of the maker or the maker's family, but in the food-producing societies division of labour means that each producer has to interact with others in order to obtain the full range of necessities; production becomes a social enterprise in which people with specialised abilities place them at each others' service. Also, the collective power of society takes over the task of maintaining approved claims to possession, eventually coming to use trained police and complex legal systems for the purpose. The wealthy individuals, who stand out so boldly in the societies of domination, do so just because they do not depend on their individual abilities alone but benefit from the powers of the collectivity. Although immediate appearances suggest the contrary, in economic life individualism is weaker and collectivism stronger in the societies of Domination than among the Expedient communities. The division of labour marked the beginning of reliance upon co-operation in economic affairs.

The food the Expedient people lived on cost them only the effort of taking it, and the literature speaks repeatedly of the large amounts of free time they enjoyed, Service calling them the most leisured people in the world[1]. Farmers live in a different way. Their food, especially before the introduction of powered machinery, has cost a great deal of effort; in order to rely upon a continuing supply they need to be secure in the exclusive use of land as well as tools, and the new society was able to provide this where the first communities could not. With the advent of farming, government, sedentary life and the surplus that came with them, both the extent and the effectiveness of ownership leapt beyond all former bounds, advancing towards the condition we know, where it can almost be said that everything on the planet is owned by some person or group, and not just nominally but with support from society that enables them to impose conditions on others for the use of their property. The necessities of

---

[1]Service 1966, 13

life became commodities to be owned, bought and sold, and the occasional barter of the Expedient communities grew into the market. Domination-by-ownership proved so powerful and pervasive that as chattel slavery it was extended even to people.

One can of course conceptually separate farming from social domination and many a designer of anarchistic utopias has done so. Historically, however, they come together. When doctors treat their patients, masters manage their servants, officers command their soldiers, rulers manipulate their officials and farmers deal with their crops their detailed actions have little in common, but the pattern of behaviour is the same in each case: one level super-imposed upon another and dominating it. It is a pattern pervading the societies which produce their own food but playing hardly any part in the Expedient communities.

In their economic activities members of the Expedient communities enjoy almost total freedom from social restrictions, the limitations they suffer being imposed by the natural world; Ituri pygmies may join in the hunt or go off to gather roots as the whim takes them. The societies of Domination, even the least developed of them, function in a different way; any who would live as Nuer must give the needs of the cattle precedence over their personal inclinations, and with further development the requirements to be met become more specific, the socially-imposed limitations more severe.

In the political-intellectual sphere change moves in the opposite direction, independent individuality strengthening as society develops. In the Expedient communities no distinct mechanism for imposing political-intellectual uniformity appeared, but this was because political-intellectual independence hardly appeared among them – it is probably not going too far to say that it remained inconceivable – and when a tendency is not present no means of restraining it are required. The presence of institutions designed to maintain or enforce particular systems of belief indicates awareness of dissension, and it is only in more sophisticated societies that such institutions are found.

The transition from communities of Expedience to societies of Domination entails two parallel but converse movements. In economic-material life, from individualism towards collectivism; in political-intellectual from collectivism towards individualism.

Many an explorer found the Expedient peoples willing to fight, but they did so sporadically, responding to the immediate circumstances, while the society displacing them accepts a degree of systematic militarisation as an established feature of its organisation. In organised warfare the two-layer pattern appears once more, each combatant state seeking to subjugate or to avoid being subjugated – objectives unknown among the Expedient communities – by means of formed bodies of troops, each of them, once the simplest stage has been passed, under its officers. Pointing out that a hierarchical society, even a chiefdom, can make war more effectively than the hit-and-run bands of the headless communities, Service notes that they also have greater potential for making peace. The society of Domination replaces endemic, small-scale violence with a contest aiming at a peace in which the balance of power has been shifted[1].

In their writings on military history Keegan and Holmes show how primitive warfare differs from conflicts between states. It tends to be an endemic condition of raid and ambush, its object less to achieve a victory than to assert separate identity. Although weaker tribes may yield space to the stronger, "of outright conquest and occupation there is no trace[2]." Anything approaching a formal encounter takes the form of ritualised display before an audience, a death or even a serious wound being the signal for peace to break out. Fighting of this type does not extend far beyond the Expedient stage; warfare between Nuer and Dinka had already become a serious affair, and some of the earliest writings tell of Sumerian and Egyptian armies fighting, like modern forces, in order to break the opponent's will to resist; in the terms we are using here, either to establish domination or to defeat an attempt at imposing it.

---

[1]Service 1975, 271
[2]Keegan and Holmes 1985, 206-7

Societies of Domination tend to occupy their territory more solidly than the Expedient peoples with their sparse populations ever could, and to spread as it were sideways until encountering another group similarly spreading from another centre. When the two societies possess approximately equal strength an uneasy border results, but an imbalance (more common) leads one to ride up over the other. When the political structure of the conquered group is retained this constitutes the transition from chieftainship, where the head rules directly over the people, to kingship, in which the ruler works through one or more levels of subordinate authority. The process was repeated, the kings in turn being subjected to the king of kings, and Domination eventually reached its peak in the world-spanning empires of modern times.

Empires and imperialism have been favourite targets of the reformers and revolutionaries for most of this century, but the theories attempting to account for them offer surprisingly little help to one trying to grasp their place in the historical development of society. Of those discussed, for example, in Mommsen's *Theories of Imperialism*, only Schumpeter's is said to take in any of the early empires, and that only those of Rome and Persia. Most of them are no more than variations on themes introduced by Marx or Lenin, and nearly all confine themselves to the period after about 1830. It is almost as if the Incas, China, Sumer and Assyria, Ghana, Mali, Songhay and Bornu, the Arab, Mongol and Ottoman empires had never existed. The limitation seems to be one consequence of the view that capitalist productive relations form the substance of existing society, other features being little more than secondary consequences of these. The pre-capitalist empires have almost dropped out of the sight of the theoreticians, and this continues even though the persistence of capitalism after the virtual disappearance of the empires has invalidated Lenin's view of imperialism as the highest (and final) stage of capitalism. Michael Doyle's *Imperialism* pays greater attention to more modern theorists, but mentions none who trace empires farther back than Bismarck, Disraeli or "European industrialism." Schumpeter's view is more inclusive than most, but even he falls short of full integration linking the ancient forces with modern capitalism only as a historical residue which corrupts it[1].

Modern imperialism can of course be given a definition that separates it from earlier versions; each empire, for that matter, can be shown to differ, and not just in trivial ways, from every other. No definition ever will enable us to say with certainty and exactitude, of every candidate for the title, whether it ranks or not, for no social construct ever has been an empire and nothing else, and every empire throughout its life has been in transition from a pre- to a post-imperial phase. Among the ethno-historians one's empire is another's state[2]. The category has fuzzy edges and internal irregularities, but so do others, "men" and "women" for example; they are none the less put to fruitful use, in serious study as well as in everyday life.

The theory being presented here needs no *ad hoc* additions to account for either empires or imperialism. The ideology of Principle (its presence will be accounted for later) leads its adherents to seek domination or submission according to circumstances, and they have been displaying this dual tendency over the whole period covered by the written record. In the dim light thrown by the first known writing, that of Sumer about 3,500 B.C., what looms out of the shadows is already an empire. To treat the empires of the Nineteenth Century as a species not known before is to create an artificial problem, for Domination, tending towards empire, has been with us since structured society first appeared. What we have to explain, rather, is how any one dominating group should find itself restricted to a particular area, and we do this by reference first to the presence of competing groups and second to the difficulties raised by distance and geography; as technology overcame these so the empires came to extend over most parts of the earth, each of them restricted mainly by the others.

An empire arises as an explicated embodiment of the ideology of Principle. Differences between its two main layers are heavily stressed, the rulers presented as the embodiment of

---

[1] Doyle 1986, 19,23
[2] Service 1975, 193

duty, responsibility and justice, the subject peoples as willful and childlike, incapable of seeing beyond the convenience of the moment and needing to be restrained for their own good. The practices adopted go to maintain the firmness of the distinction, the administrators usually being marked off from their subjects by language, costume, education, religion, diet and customs, and sometimes also by skin-colour. The emperor commonly remains far away; Queen Victoria, ruler of the greatest of empires, visited no overseas part of it except Ireland. An empire tends to set a rigid ceiling on the upward mobility of subject peoples, so that ambitious indigenes seeking full domination for themselves can achieve it only by overthrowing their masters. They did this often enough through history, the outcome through long ages being the replacement (not always immediate) of one empire by another.

From its first appearance social domination grew. Starting with headmen and chiefs it slowly strengthened through tyrants, kings and kings of kings, suffering only local and temporary setbacks, until it climaxed in the worldwide empires. The British Empire reached its maximum extension in 1933[1], when most of the world was incorporated in one empire or another. At that point, with the few who ruled the empires having most of humanity as their subjects, Domination came close to attaining the pyramidal structure towards which it had tended since its first appearance. But in England with the Civil War, in Europe with the French Revolution, in other parts of the world somewhat later, there entered the hero who was eventually to overcome not just this or that empire but imperialism itself.

---

[1]Morris 1981, 316-7

After the Empires

EACH empire had its enemies, but serious resistance to the principle of imperialism did not arise until late in the Eighteenth Century, when the *sans-culottes* erupted against the *aristos* – both groups defined by political attachment rather than rank or income, the *aristos* often plebeians and the *sans-culottes* wearers of revolutionary trousers instead of reactionary knee-breeches[1]. Revolutionary France proclaimed a new age of freedom, equality and brotherhood, nations as well as people to be liberated, but the impulse was not followed through; Napoleon re-established French imperialism and only in the Twentieth Century did the age of the empires come to an end. After 1789 they had still a century and more to go, but well before their end a new form of political life had begun to move within them.

Each major ideology to join those already exercising public influence comes largely as a corrective for the failures of its predecessor; these being limited to particular areas (had failure been general the society would not have survived) the incomer exhibits uneven development. One group sets to work on this difficulty and (perhaps later) another on that, and the ideology makes its appearance in localised spasms, apparently disconnected. Not until well into the Nineteenth Century did the ideology following that of Principle achieve coherent formulation and political expression in the liberal movement, although its appearance in particular fields can be traced back to the Sixteenth at least. Protestantism, with its elevation of private judgment against dogma and obedience, was beginning to call the domination of established principles into question, and although Anglicanism was to settle down as an established national church the new impulse was not lost. It survived, largely underground, to burst out again in the multiple sects of the Civil War period and to spread beyond religious activities. In the following centuries opponents falling in the political struggle ceased to be executed or even impeached, hours of labour were restricted, the penal-

---

[1]Cobban 1956, 14

110

ties for crime rendered less severe, and police with limited weaponry, or sometimes unarmed, replaced the military as a peace-keeping force. Minorities came to be tolerated. The tendency is sometimes called democracy (though that term also has other meanings) and it consists generally in the establishment, among the conventions of the society, of one to the effect that those who wield its power shall do so with restraint. John Stuart Mill made the classic statement:

> The object of this Essay is to assert one very simple principle, as entitled to govern absolutely the dealings of society with the individual in the way of compulsion and control, whether the means used be physical force in the form of legal penalties, or the moral coercion of public opinion. That principle is, that the sole end for which mankind are warranted, individually or collectively, in interfering with the liberty of action of any of their number, is self-protection. That the only purpose for which power can be rightfully exercised over any member of a civilized community, against his will, is to prevent harm to others. His own good, either physical or moral, is not a sufficient warrant. He cannot rightfully be compelled to do or forbear because it will be better for him to do so, because it will make him happier, because, in the opinions of others, to do so would be wise, or even right... the only part of the conduct of any one, for which he is amenable to society, is that which concerns others. In the part which merely concerns himself, his independence is, of right, absolute. Over himself, over his own body and mind, the individual is sovereign[1].

That could not have been said in the stateless Expedient communities and if permitted to appear in the societies of Domination, before tendencies towards self-limitation had

---

[1]Mill n.d. (c. 189-?), 20-21

begun to gain acceptance, it would have fallen dead from the press. In Britain in 1859 it aroused a resonance that echoes through the civilised world and still grows stronger. Between 1972 and 1987 seventeen countries – more than one each year – moved from authoritarian rule to some version of democratic government[1], and although political democracy does not amount to the condition envisaged by Mill, yet establishment of equal political rights for all is a sizeable step towards it.

The assumption underlying Mill's statement, namely that the political universe consists, or ought to consist, of multiple units of equal value, sharply defined and related to each other only by external contact, finds expression also in physical science. There it took the shape of the "billiard ball" conception of the nature of the material universe (which still plays a significant part in scientific thought). In politics and physics alike, a great point about these (assumed) particles, sharply distinct from each other, is that they can be accurately counted. What we have here is, in fact, one of the principal assumptions of the ideology of Precision.

We noted appearances of Domination in the Expedient communities and even among animals, but only with the establishment of the ideology of Principle did it become a social force. Similarly with the pursuit of Precision. Instances of this can be traced in some of the earliest writings, the Babylonians recording stellar movements and the ancient Egyptians accurately surveying their fields, while Euclid ("that precise man," as Stephen Leacock termed him) has never been surpassed on his own ground. In Renaissance Italy and Ancient Greece science accompanied the city state but it remained, as Galileo found, subject to domination[2].

In Seventeenth Century Europe, as the first efforts began to be made to establish the self-limiting conception of the state in internal affairs, such[3] scattered attempts to rationalise the apparent chaos of the physical world began to come together. Bacon's classification of the sciences provided a foundation

---

[1] Milligan 1987

[2] ¶and Bruno?

[3] ¶... affairs, ~~such~~ scattered...

for later work (it was adopted by Diderot and d'Alembert for use in the *Encyclopédie*) and the Royal Society (to be rapidly emulated in other advanced countries), was founded in 1660. More precise handling of materials had permitted the production of microscopes and telescopes, with all their consequences for the advancement of knowledge. In religion the old rough-and-ready method, believe or burn, came under attack from Friends, Shakers, Mortalists, Fifth Monarchy Men, Muggletonians and many other sects, each of them seeking to repress the domination of the Church by law established, claiming the same right of free enquiry in religion that the scientists demanded (and to some extent enjoyed) in their sphere. Priestley belonged to the Unitarians and Newton (who seems to have spent more time on religion than on any other subject) came, in private if not in public, to reject the Trinity and demote Christianity from its privileged position[1].

The ideology of Principle had produced slavery in Britain as elsewhere; during the third quarter of the Eighteenth Century this home of freedom harboured some 14,000 human beings who were the legal property of others, and even so Britain led the world by abolishing the condition at home in 1772 and in the dominions in 1834 (though a form of serfdom continued to 1838)[2]. This was due largely to the evangelical movement, an appearance of Precision in the religious field which used law as well as persuasion to induce a people with the power to own slaves to refrain from doing so, bringing the practice of Christianity into more exact agreement with its principles.

Adherents of the ideology of Precision have been appearing in Britain at least since the Sixteenth Century. In the latter half of the Nineteenth, and the early part of the Twentieth, their numbers grew to a point where the new influence began to exercise continuing restraint over Domination. Extension of the franchise to virtually all adults, the obligation upon rulers to pay serious attention to their economists and other scientific experts and the retraction of the empires, these were some of the more obvious signs indicating the rise of the ideology of Precision. Acceptance of this ideology among the

---

[1] Manuel 1973, passim
[2] Morris 1980, 33, 442

major social influences is marked by the appearance of the society of self-limitation.

Each of the two previous forms of society had its distinctive way of obtaining its material requirements and so has the new one, its method being industry which uses the results of science. With isolated appearances in earlier times, and starting to produce significant effects in the early Nineteenth Century, this began to attain maturity with mass-production, automation and computerisation. The industrial unit is not the free range of the Expedient peoples or the traditional spreading farm, limited only by other farms, of the societies of Principle, but the enclosed factory, its limiting walls functional parts of its structure. Machines require, and increasingly so as they develop, neither the speed and endurance of the hunter nor the muscle-power of the labourer, but the careful self-control of the machinist, driver or pilot, and later of the keyboard-operator. By the use of science and industry the modern advanced state acquires greater power over its environment than the communities of Expediency or the societies of Principle ever wielded, and the new abilities, won by the practice of self-restraint, bring a need for still greater limitation.

Empires and Expedient communities did not need to limit themselves, for they found more than enough limitation being imposed upon them from without by the natural environment and, upon empires, also by other empires. These external restraints are no longer so effective. Industrial civilisation has the capacity to destroy the environment on which it depends, and each great power can destroy any opponent at the risk of incurring destruction itself. (Some second-rank states are also approaching this condition, nuclear armament tending to act as an equaliser between nations as the Colt revolver was said to do between men). The most acute dangers now come not from without but from within society, and self-restraint provides the only safeguard against them. Reason shows the need for this, but (fortunately for us all) its implementation does not depend upon the persuasive powers of those who have come to understand it. Self-limitation emerges in the same way as Principle, as a phase in the course of ideological development which began when humanity gained a degree of freedom from the genetic constraints which compel the animals.

During the last four centuries (and mainly within the last two) a development has occurred comparable with the Neolithic Revolution, the organisation and practices of society changing more than they had since Akkad of Sargon established the first empire in Sumer around 3,500 BC. Starting and developing within the empires, the new growth has flowered in a new type of state which, within a few centuries (and mainly within the last fifty years), has spread over a world it had taken the empires eight thousand years to conquer.

The movements bringing this about did not, for the most part, set out with that intention. The flag each one waved was the freeing of its own people from foreign domination, and what happened to others was not their concern; Gandhi, for example, showed little interest in the sufferings of non-Indians during his years in South Africa. They set out not to end imperialism but to impose limits upon it. Still holding to the two-layer pattern (the distinctions between rulers and ruled, employers and workers, professionals and laymen have outlasted the empires) they imposed upon it a new element of firm vertical divisions limiting horizontal expansion. Each movement strove to expel the foreign overlords and establish its nation as an independent state, and as one colony after another succeeded in the attempt so the empires became increasingly under restriction, eventually to such an extent that their period may be said to have ended, to be succeeded by that of a type of state not known before. The empires had imposed limitation upon each other, but the new politics adopted it as a principle to be universalised and applied even to themselves, proclaiming the new slogan: *national self-determination*. In establishing its borders each state of the new type took the claims of adjoining states into account and, while resisting any intrusion, also refrained from encroaching on its neighbours. The expansive empire was succeeded by the self-limiting state, a structure displaying firm limits in both dimensions, each of its layers being vertically limited by the one above or below and the whole self-limited in its horizontal extension.

The old city states provided hardly more than a premonition of what was to come. In Ancient Greece the small were subject to the great, the system functioned on the dominatory principle[1], and much the same is true of Renaissance Italy, the "liberta" celebrated by the Florentine citizen looking very like imperialism to inhabitants of Pisa, Livorno and other cities subjugated by Florence[2].

There were probably no perfect empires, none in which all members of the subject peoples were fully reconciled to their position, and it is unlikely that there ever was a perfect hunter-gatherer community, one doing nothing at all to husband or increase its resources. Equally, there is no such thing as the perfect self-limiting state, but to the extent that this condition is achieved the political world comes to consist of units which accord their neighbours the independence they demand for themselves.

The societies of Domination with their expansionist tendencies produced war, and the great empires the great wars. A primary cause of the Second World War was the attempt of Germany and Japan, and later Italy, to establish themselves alongside the greater empires, and the main military conflicts since then have been of three types, all of them after-effects of expanding domination. First, the struggle (conducted largely by proxy), in Vietnam and elsewhere between the USSR and the USA, motivated by the fear of each that the other was seeking to extend its dominion, tending to behave not as a self-limiting state but as an empire. Second, attempts to hold on to some remnant of empire, examples being the French struggles in Algeria and Indo-China, the British adventures in Suez and the Falklands and their continued presence in Northern Ireland. Third, attempts by imperial or formerly imperial powers to prevent new states establishing themselves, the Arab-Israeli conflict being one prominent example and the resistance to oppression of the blacks in South Africa (a movement not limited to blacks) perhaps the beginnings of another new creation. The association of the great wars with

---

[1]Finlay 1958, 78
[2]Ralph 1973, 48

the great empires, and of war generally with the societies of Domination, is strong enough and close enough to suggest that the spreading repression of this ideology by that of self-limitation will tend towards repression also of the factors making for war.

The new type of state comes complete with its own problems. Trying to maintain conditions in which a variety of ethnic and linguistic groups can live without one imposing itself upon the others, it finds them struggling, some for domination and others for independence, while the socialist, communist and anarchist movements, ideologically barred from quietly accepting either divisions between nations or domination of one group by another, press for a more united and more egalitarian society. Other groups strive in other directions, and not all of them are reasonable, democratic or pacifistic; the self- limiting state is unlikely to lead a peaceful life. But internal struggle, terrorism, and even civil war should it come to that, differ from a continuation of the imperial wars in being less likely to threaten the survival of the race.

The ideology of Precision, inclining its adherents towards close examination of conditions and restraining expansive tendencies, endows societies developing it with a greatly increased ability to perceive limits before crashing into them, often making it possible to avoid or soften the encounter. The empires benefited from this development in their last days, they did not all continue blindly on in every colony until they came into head-on collision with the movements seeking independence, and the nuclear super-powers behave with great caution towards each other. When a natural species meets conditions that allow it to expand, it tends to increase in numbers until its very success brings disaster, but the nations are already beginning to limit their populations. The increasing powers wielded by modern technology threaten irreparable damage to the environment on which we depend, but a growing movement urges restraint. Self-limitation appears in other fields beside the directly political structure of the new type of state.

Empires changed the states they took over, driving them forward so that changes which in the first instance had taken millennia occupied only centuries, or even decades. The Romans had this effect upon the more northern European peoples and Europe in turn spurred Africa and America into acceleration. As Herbert Luethy has expressed it, "That which today stands up against colonial domination is itself the work of colonizers[1]." Even with assistance from those who have traveled the route before, the transition from one form of society to another never comes easily, and the changes entailed never come as unqualified benefits. It is not at all clear yet that the independence achieved by the former colonies has in all cases improved the condition of their people, although it has certainly demonstrated some limitations of the Marxist thesis that advanced capitalist powers need empire over backward countries for their own future development. The empires have virtually gone, but advanced technology roars ahead while the newly independent states drop farther behind[2].

These developments have of course been recognised and studied (though not, to my knowledge, in the context given them here) and attempts have been made, as they have been made with the society of Domination, to explain them as a consequence of technological progress. Examination of this alleged cause reveals its supposed effects already present within it; the industry and weaponry accompanying the emergence of the self-limiting state could not have arisen without the theorising of the scientists and although this, like all thinking leading to substantial novelty, embraces spontaneity, "wild cards" and intuitive leaps, yet the part of it more directly responsible for the new products is marked by a rigorous precision requiring intense self-control, which is to say self-limitation. As the production of food and the political features of the society that emerged together with it are best understood as expressions of the one major ideology, that of Principle, so the military and industrial developments that have come with the self-limiting state, and the distinctive political features of that state, are best understood as expressing the ideology of Precision.

---

[1]Quoted in Mommsen 1981, 77-78
[2]Mommsen 1981, 144-5

The Eidodynamic

SINCE introducing Walsby's ascription of the ideologies of Expediency, Domination and Precision to the eidostatic and those of Reform, Revolution and Repudiation to the eidodynamic, I have spoken only of the first three. We found each of these established as the distinctive mark of a stage in social development, but the same cannot be said of the eidodynamic ones; although the socialist, communist and anarchist movements exercise influence, the social practices they advocate remain mainly aspirations.

Isolated expressions of eidodynamic assumptions can be traced far back into history, Walsby finding them in ancient Greek and Chinese writings[1], but they can hardly be said to have motivated political activities before the appearance of the Diggers and other egalitarian protesters of Seventeenth Century England. In the French Revolution Babeuf and followers, with their communistic Utopia, claim a place among the eidodynamics, but the main movement has to be ascribed to the ideology of precision. Not until the Nineteenth Century did the reformers and revolutionaries come to form enduring parties and movements.

These have not been able to realise their own idea of themselves; claiming to represent the interests of the great body of the people against a dominant and exploitative few, and therefore expecting to receive overwhelming numerical support, they have remained in the minority. They have known war and peace, boom and slump, the virtual disappearance of empires and ruling monarchs, the growth of political democracy, general education, widespread literacy and mass communications; one of them has been able to grasp control of governmental power in two of the largest states and a number of smaller ones. Each of these conditions has been proclaimed, before the event, the one thing needed to bring the great body of the people to accept socialism (or communism or anarchism) but none of them have produced this effect. The features and tendencies these groups oppose – private ownership, together-

---

[1] Walsby n.d.(c.196-?)

ness, economic competition, institutional religion, hierarchy, authority, low valuation of theory, respect for success in life, willingness to defend the national group – these continue to be the values by which society mainly operates.

Neither Reform nor Revolution has anywhere brought the changes sought. There have been no societies on even a national scale which were anarchist or communist as those terms were understood by the founders of the movements, and enquiry into the states sometimes called socialist soon shows their socialism to be hardly more than a verbal cosmetic, thinly spread over a mainly eidostatic substance. Under Stalin collectivist forms of organisation were forcibly imposed on Russian agriculture, but individual interest remains the driving force of the economy there as elsewhere. In her study of the way a Soviet collective farm operates Caroline Humphrey notes that although in official meetings, whether of the Communist Party, the collective farm or the local soviet, one is required to deny that people work mainly for themselves, in fact everybody does so[1].

When the British Labour Party has had control of the powers of government the socialists within it have not been able to convince a majority of the electorate of the desirability and practicality of socialism; after each experiment with Labour the country has returned towards its old ways like a stretched rubber band relaxing. Between 1945 and 1979 several Labour governments introduced changes intended as moves towards socialism, but the response of the intended beneficiaries was to elect, three times running, a government more harshly anti-socialist than any this century.

The enduring attachment of the great majority to the eidostatic ideologies defeats the efforts of the eidodynamics to set up their intended society, and even when revolutions occur they produce results different from those expected by the revolutionaries. The return of the USSR towards private ownership and political pluralism, and the indications that China is set on the same course, suggest the workings of an influence deeper than any 'betrayal of the revolution,' or even

---

[1]Humphrey 1983, 191-2

any particular set of social conditions, and this receives confirmation when we find revolutions in non-political activities following a pattern similar to that of the political ones. I turn for an example to the course of development followed by physical science, as presented by Thomas Kuhn in his book *The Structure of Scientific Revolutions*. (The fact that Kuhn wrote, as far as I know, without having heard of systematic ideology, increases the value of his work for our purposes).

Before any observation or experimental result can carry meaning it has to be set against a picture of the world (or at least the part of the world the discipline covers), and its significance varies with the background chosen. The phenomena associated with burning meant one thing to chemists while they held the phlogiston theory and something else after Priestley (or Lavoisier or Hales or Scheele) discovered oxygen and the observation that the sun rises acquired a different significance as Copernicus's work came to be accepted. Kuhn terms such scientific world-pictures "paradigms," and studies the process by which one comes to displace another in the thinking of the scientific community.

No paradigm exactly fits all the evidence; over time anomalies accumulate and eventually one investigator, for the major shifts a Copernicus, Newton, Lavoisier or Einstein, introduces a new paradigm which succeeds in integrating them, or in doing so in a more satisfying way. These innovators seldom act with revolutionary intent; like other workers in the field they seek a more precise correlation between theory and observation and the upheaval resulting from their work is usually as unwanted by them as by others. Radical innovation receives no better welcome in science than in society at large, the new paradigm commonly having to wait for general acceptance until one generation of investigators in the field has been replaced by another.

Such upsets, substantially changing ideas, explosively releasing accumulated tensions, arousing resistance and bitter resentment, well deserve to be called revolutions, but they do not indicate any deep changes in the ideological structure of the scientific community. The generation accepting the new ideas emulates its predecessors in supporting (what has now become) the authoritative view and goes on to render it more precise and secure. The eidodynamics may stress the revolutionary content in the achievements of the great innovators but the eidostatic majority (to the extent that it thinks of them at all) accepts their work in a version shaped by its own assumptions, turning them into establishment personalities issuing authoritative pronouncements in much the same way as their predecessors. Their own behaviour serves to confirm this view, for rather than going on to stir things up even more they tend to settle down as the new authorities in their respective fields. Freud, for example, would allow none of his followers to carry through any revolutions within psychoanalysis; Jung, and others unable to accept the orthodox views, found themselves excluded.

This points the distinction between ideas, in the sense of specific beliefs, and the broad assumptions which, in their sets, form the bases from which the great ideologies arise. A paradigm shift entails changes in the particular ideas of the scientific community – ideas about the place of the earth in the stellar universe, or the indivisibility of the atom, or the source from which the sun derives its energy – but on the more general issues involved in all these particular ones, such as the parts properly to be played by authority and independent critical thought respectively in determining which beliefs should be held, both the innovators and the great majority of workers in the discipline continue to display attitudes which are eidostatic rather than eidodynamic. In the terms we were using earlier they retain the eidostatic ethos: in Walsby's terms the content of their thinking has changed while its form remains largely unaffected.

Other events commonly described as revolutions also display these features. The railway, the internal combustion engine and powered flight all produced revolutions in transport, but neither those who use these facilities nor those who introduced the changes are thereby shown to have departed from eidostatic modes of thought. Each of these introductions depends for its successful functioning upon what Kuhn distinguishes as normal (i.e. non-revolutionary) science and technology, and also upon the continuing presence of an established society working largely by rote to provide a steady supply of trained people and material resources. In other fields of activity too, in housing, household equipment, entertainment, communications and sport, in philosophy and education, one reform or revolution succeeds another, each of them indicating or producing changes in the particular ideas of those involved but not in the deeper assumptions that define them as Expedient, Principled or Precise on the one hand or Reformers, Revolutionaries or Repudiators on the other. Kuhn's scenario does not agree with the expectations of the political revolutionaries but it does, better than those expectations, fit the course that revolutions have so far followed, in technology, politics and general society as well as science.

Establishment of a socialist society would require substantial changes in popular atittudes. The socialist movement has demonstrated, over generations, its inability to effect these, and this has induced some observers to move on to a more strenuous but (they believe) more effective way of working. These become communists, they set out to bring about a revolution which shall reverse the positions of the classes, establishing a dictatorship of the proletariat and therewith, they expect, what we would describe as the predominance of the eidodynamic. But revolutionary communism does not reach its goal either. The states ruled by communist movements hardly come closer to realising eidodynamic intentions than the professedly capitalist ones, and the great majority of the people who on Marxist theory ought to be inclined towards supporting the activities of the communists persist in preferring their present condition. Events in the "communist" countries show the eidostatics maintaining their numerical superiority, and consequently their predominating influence upon social practices, even through revolution.

When revolutionaries gain control of the state they may be able to secure formal compliance with new ways of working, replace private holdings by collective farms, substitute Mao or Stalin for the Emperor or the Tsar as the father of his people, and impose a new public rhetoric, but they do not succeed in importing their own dynamic impulse to the general body of the people. Rather do they themselves become absorbed in an effort to establish the new ideas, moving, in their practice if not in their intentions, back from the eidodynamic to the eidostatic. In sending the Red Army across the ice to attack the Kronstadt sailors Trotsky acted by the same ethos as Wellington ordering the Guards forward at Waterloo.

With revolutionaries as with reformers, some persist in trying to make headway along the familiar path while others attempt a more demanding but (they believe) more promising route. These become anarchists, interpreting the failure of their previous efforts (or of the observed efforts of others) as evidence that freedom can be achieved only by doing away with all imposed authority, that of revolutionaries along with the rest, since authority is itself the source of social limitations. The liberated society can be achieved, anarchists believe, only as an assembly of autonomous people. This approach also has so far failed to achieve its object, and we have no grounds for expecting it to be more successful in future.

Although the ideological series finds its most familiar expression in the range of political parties, it is of course not the case that each anarchist has been a communist, each communist a socialist and so on. People often work through much of the ideological range without overt political commitment, entering the party-political system only at some advanced stage if at all, and this directs our attention to a feature not yet mentioned.

Human beings live within a dual environment, one aspect of it predominantly social although never losing its natural base, the other predominantly natural although becoming increasingly socialised. In the course of movement along the ideological range attitudes towards these undergo a reversal.

Members of the Expedient communities accept their social environment unquestioningly, their attention remaining fastened upon the natural world. In the societies of Domination this balance of attention, though retained, undergoes modification, the organisation and maintenance of society receiving more critical attention and the natural world correspondingly less. Considerable numbers come to be engaged in religion, the military, education and administration, activities not required so long as existing social conditions were taken for granted. In hard times the people are likely to vent their displeasure on their rulers, an option not open to the headless expedient communities.

Societies of self-limitation move farther along the same road. Here producers seldom approach the material world directly, acting instead mainly through the social media of science and technology. "Service" industries (that is, those dealing with intra- rather than extra-social relationships) take up an increasing amount of time and attention, and consumers come to depend upon socially purified water, socially modified crops, socially produced clothes and houses and socially approved building sites. In setting up these conditions society accepts increasing responsibility for the welfare of its members; henceforward, if drought brings famine or an earthquake shatters the town the disaster will be ascribed at least partly to a social failure. Greater reserves should have been carried; the town should not have been built on a fault-line. But the failure is assumed to be correctable within the existing social structure.

Up to this point identification with the social environment prevails, existing arrangements being first taken for granted (Expediency), then defended (Principle) then improved (Precision). These changes indicate a growing awareness of wider possibilities, but the main source of trouble and suffering is still located outside the society. With the next step this changes, the shift marking the transition from the eidostatic to the eidodynamic.

Our enquiry began with a brief survey of the major political parties and some of their principal ideological features, namely the extent and depth of the changes sought, the preference for freedom or control in economic and political affairs respectively, and the value placed upon theory as a guide to action. Non-politicals, conservatives and liberals alike value the main features of existing society; the changes sought even by the liberals are intended to perfect what exists. All the eidostatic ideologies prefer individualism to collectivism in economic affairs, collectivism to individualism in political matters; they all favour, that is to say, private enterprise and patriotism. They all value practice and experience above theory as guides to action. Along the range from non-political to liberal these features weaken, but[1] with the further transition to socialism a reversal takes place. The eidodynamic ideologies prefer collectivism to individualism in economic affairs and individualism to collectivism in political matters; they all favour common ownership of the means of production and value independent critical thinking above any obligation to Queen, country or flag. They value theory above practice and experience as a guide to action.

Where the eidostatic ideologies had directed their attention mainly outward, even liberalism accepting private enterprise and hierarchy (although seeking a greater place for merit and achievement), socialism proposes to improve the human condition by a fundamental reformation of society. No longer is the source of our troubles located in the outer world; now it is by directing our efforts inward, towards the construction of a more egalitarian and humane society, that we shall overcome our difficulties.

As the existing social structure comes to be cast in the role of villain, so the natural world is deprived of its power to harm and ceases to need so much attention; the problem of production, socialists sometimes say, has been solved. The unregenerate human afflicted with original sin becomes the noble savage, children no longer need the rod and education shifts from the instilling of knowledge and training in approved conduct to the encouragement of self-expression. Claiming to speak for the ordinary people, or the workers, the eidodynamics present them as the embodiment of normal, healthy, natural life in opposition to the artificial, restrictive, death-directed tendencies of class-divided society.

This transference of critical attention from the natural to the social finds expression, even more clearly than in the sequence of orthodox parties, in the movement first known as ecological or conservationist and now increasingly as "the greens." In promoting the interests of the natural environment the greens began, like Robert Owen and the other early

---

[1] ¶... weaken, ~~but~~ and with...

socialists, by expecting that once the dangers of what was happening had been made clear the authorities would take the necessary steps; in this case, controlling the farmers, together with the makers of pesticides and artificial fertilisers, protecting threatened species and preventing industry wrecking what remains of the natural ecology. This approach still continues, but the lack of satisfactory response has provoked some of the greens into more aggressive methods; these now appeal directly to the voters, demonstrate at sensitive sites and sometimes resist the police sent to disperse them. In some cases the development amounts almost to a transfer of allegiance from society to the natural world, completing the reversal we spoke of earlier. Where the expedient communities killed animals without restraint that people might live some of the extremist greens, setting fire-bombs in stores that sell furs, risk killing people to protect animals. The movement has begun to acquire the same threefold structure as the eidodynamic movement in party politics and in the same way, the failure of one method provoking a more radical undertaking which turns out to enjoy even less support, and consequently to have even less chance of attaining its declared objectives, than the previous one.

The pattern of development being displayed by the green movement shows that progression through the successive eidodynamic stages does not appear only among the orthodox parties; it is an ideological process, not merely a political one. The greens show no more awareness of this than do the older movements, seeing themselves rather as advocating a return to basic principles which have been neglected in the drive for profit and power. They hold up the example set by the original communities, which lived for far longer than our own civilisation has endured, perhaps for millions of years, without seriously damaging their environment. In doing this, however, they omit a major factor, namely the difference between the powers wielded by the early people and those available now. In order to conserve the environment on which it depends our society needs to exert massive self-restraint, and there is no good reason to believe that the early communities were doing this. I drew attention in an earlier chapter to the behaviour of

European Paleolithics, and the early Pacific peoples were no more restrained. In Hawaii they had eliminated at least forty species of birds before Europeans arrived, while the Maoris burned the New Zealand forests and, within fifty years of their arrival, had destroyed the fur seal rookeries of North Island and all thirteen species of flightless moas, as well as twenty types of flying birds[1]. If earlier societies did not do as much damage as our own it was because they had not the power. Far from having initiated destruction of the environment our society is the first to have imposed restraints upon such activity.

To see the changes advocated by the greens as a return to earlier or more natural practices is to get things back to front. Their proposals constitute an advance towards a condition in which society accepts responsibility for the environment, something it has never done before. And the same applies, of course, to the directly political movements; anarchists, in particular, sometimes see their movement as an attempted return towards an earlier and more natural condition, but an anarchist is one who knowingly rejects authority and the state, while the original communities had yet to encounter them; anarchists and expedients stand at opposite ends of a long process of development.

With each step along the ideological range the analysis of society put forward becomes sharper and the thinking more highly organised; as this happens so numerical support falls off. The progression from reform through revolution to repudiation has been in effect, though not in intention, a flight into theory. At the eidodynamic extreme the purist anarcho-socialists of the SPGB declare ideas all-important; the future of society depends, they claim, upon acceptance of their theories by a majority. Driven to this stance by the demonstrated futility of attempts to bring about the required changes by more directly practical methods, anarchism receives even less support than communism (as that enjoys less than socialism). The flight into theory brings the repudiators of existing society face-to-face with the immediate source of all the frustrations suffered

---

[1]Mitchell 1990

by the eidodynamics: the presence of a massive and enduring majority of eidostatics. Most people experience their society as freedom rather than limitation. They support society against the natural world, do not feel themselves oppressed or exploited by the system, value experience above theory as a guide to action, and show more inclination to oppose substantial changes in the deep structure of society than to favour them. There are no good reasons for expecting this to change.

The Origins of Ideologies

HAVING looked very briefly at the major ideologies and some of their effects on the history and present functioning of society, we now turn to trace out their origins. In doing this we shall need two concepts which Walsby developed beyond their usual significance: *assumption* (which we have already met) and *limitation*.

I have been speaking almost entirely of societies, movements, parties and occupational groupings, and in order to understand the behaviour of these we need to study mainly their respective ideologies. The effects of individual personality cannot be entirely ruled out – the personal qualities of Sir Winston Churchill and Richard Nixon, for example, have to be taken into account when studying the history of their respective parties – but they play a minor part, seldom producing more than temporary kinks in a course whose direction is set by ideology. Any group formed of people moved by a common purpose, whether in politics or any other field of activity, is primarily an ideological entity.

Individual people, as well as groups, behave differently according to the assumptions they accept, but we cannot describe people as ideological entities without adding severe qualifications. Ideology affects only purposeful behaviour, and much that individual people do falls under other heads. They get cross, hungry, tired or sleepy, fall in love, lose their tempers, grow old, fall ill, prefer thrillers to romances (or vice versa), tend to like (or dislike) people who resemble their parents, and all without intention. Much personal conduct is governed by physical, physiological and psychological factors; in studying individual people ideologically we study only one influence among others, and one which often plays a minor role. But although people differ from groups no rigid distinction can be drawn; an ideology is a set of assumptions and assumptions are made by people, an ideological group coming into being when the assumptions made by two or more men, women or children overlap.

When acting with purpose, whether in groups or independently, we have to take the circumstances into account but we never know, with complete precision and absolute certainty, what these may be. They commonly include both things and people; we do not know, exactly, the fundamental nature of matter, and people are constantly responding in unexpected ways. If we wait for exhaustive knowledge before moving we shall not act at all; purposeful action becomes possible only when (perhaps after close examination) we *assume* circumstances to be thus or thus, and different assumptions produce different actions. Of two runners who encounter what seems to be a brick wall one assumes it to be a real wall and alters course to go around it while the other, assuming it to be a paper imitation, goes to break through. When acting with purpose we act in relation to the world as *we assume it to be*, and we become better able to predict how other people and groups will act as we learn more about their assumptions. A primary function of systematic ideology is to help us understand, for some of the assumptions which most widely and deeply influence behaviour in social affairs, how large groups of people come to make those they do and not others, and what changes in them can reasonably be expected.

To make an assumption is to accept the reality of something, of some object, person, event, thought, principle, condition or whatever, and an important part of being real is the ability to offer resistance. To accept the reality of something other than oneself is to recognise the presence of something capable of offering resistance to one's efforts, and whatever offers resistance imposes a limitation. To make an assumption, therefore, is to accept a limitation. We never do this with full spontaneity but always under pressure, accepting one limitation only in order to overcome a greater one; this theme was developed by Harold Walsby in his *Domain of Ideologies*:

> Even when we willingly submit or subject ourselves to some limitation or other (as, of course, we are constantly doing) we do so only in so far as we think this subjection enables us to overcome a greater limitation. For instance, we willingly submit to the limitations imposed upon us in the getting of food in order to avoid

> the greater limitation imposed upon us by the internal stimulus of hunger. In fact, every successful action must be based on the acceptance of certain limitations... which then become the means of overcoming the greater limitations otherwise suffered[1].

By trying constantly to minimise the limitations suffered we show ourselves to be seeking a condition entirely without limitations, and to seek something implies an assumption of its existence. Implied in all our volitional behaviour is the assumption of a condition of being absolutely unlimited, undetermined, unhindered; in short, a condition of being absolutely free, and Walsby identifies this as the *absolute assumption*. This is, he says, "our fundamental, our most permanent and primitive assumption, that into which all other assumptions must be assimilated, and that which constitutes the basis for the whole ideological structure of assumptions[2]."

The absolute assumption becomes established as the base of the ideological structure in the beginning of life. From the moment of conception the new human being lives in conditions that perfectly meet its requirements, not needing to eat or even to breathe, having all its wants met before it can feel a need. At one with its surroundings, free of any distinction between them and itself, it suffers no limitation from them. Being in complete identity with its universe it has no option but to assume itself subject to no restraints whatever, unbounded, omnipresent, omnipotent. In the later stages of intrauterine life this begins to change as the developing affective system allows perception of stimuli from the outer world, and with the trauma of birth new limitations come crashing in[3].

At first those looking after the newborn try to maintain it in the condition of the foetus, keeping it warm and clean and fed without effort on its part, but as the child grows

---

[1] Walsby 1947, 190-191

[2] Walsby 1947, 183-184. See also Appendix B. below.

[3] ¶[Para] In the later stages of intrauterine life ~~this begins to change~~ enables the absolute assumption begins to [illegible] as the developing affective system ~~allows~~ enables perception of stimuli from the outer world, and with the trauma of birth new limitations come crashing in.

this supportiveness diminishes and it comes to experience[1] the helpless dependence that adults regard as the truth of its condition. It finds itself in an intolerable position, convinced of its absolute freedom yet subject to limitations, and the only means of escape is to accept other limitations in place of those being suffered. In order to overcome those imposed by being stationary, for example, it has to take on, to assume, those entailed in motion.

As the infant grows it sometimes gets left to indicate its needs, and by crying for what it wants it shows itself to be accepting the assumption that the outside world is capable of affecting it. In doing this it accepts a massive limitation upon its assumed freedom and thereby becomes able, to some extent, to manipulate the external world in order to overcome the limitations experienced; by crying it gets fed – and assumes the limitations that come with that condition.

Through its earliest and most impressionable period the child finds warmth, food and comfort, partial confirmations of the absolute assumption, within the group of which it forms part (I shall call this the home group) while as it becomes aware of stimulations and provocations – the nasty things that impose the greater limitations – it finds them coming mainly from outside. This results in the growth of friendly feelings towards its home group and of hostile tendencies towards the world – human, social, natural and material – outside. (Walsby terms the world external to the home group the *cosmos*, and defines the condition which develops as one of positive group identification and negative cosmic identification). The behaviour of children shows them accepting the familiar as a secure base from which they venture into surroundings seen as at least potentially hostile; the "lost" child, one detached from its home group, has long been a classic figure of woe. The connotations of "group" and "cosmos" change with experience, but nobody ever quite abandons the distinction between "us" (good) and "them" (bad).

In early childhood there is of course no grasp of abstractions like "society" or "nature," and no firm or clear distinction

---

[1] ¶in part at least,

between people and things. The supportive mother becomes a nasty thing when she has to correct the child and consolation may be sought in cuddling a doll or even a blanket. Stories of talking animals and walking tables occasion no sharp surprise. The differing identifications with group and cosmos influence behaviour, but the two categories are defined expediently rather than rationally, things which produce pleasant sensations tending to be included in the home group and their contraries to be excluded from it.

Children use the material world almost wholly for their personal satisfaction, acting towards it as individualists. When handling ideas they follow the opposite path, tending to comply with the group in which they find themselves, seldom taking any independent stand. They can hardly be said to theorise. Add to these tendencies the absence of any recognition by children of change as a universal process and we have the main features of the ideology of Expediency. The ethos displayed by children confirms this; they tend strongly to follow the impulse of the moment and to do things in the easiest way they know (which is not always what adult experience shows to be the least effortful way). The primal ideology superimposes itself upon the absolute assumption. Originating in early childhood it is none the less not a childish ideology; we also learn to walk and speak in childhood, and nobody regards these as childish activities. It arises from modification of the absolute assumption in response to conditions encountered by all children, and accordingly all children come to exhibit it. On emerging from the family into independent life the scope for further development varies according to the features of the particular society, one of the most important being its ideological structure.

The Expedient ideology imposes the minimum of command and prohibition. This does not, however, constitute effective freedom of action, for the impulse of the moment can be followed only so far as circumstances permit, the impulse towards eating, for example, only when food can be had. When tempted to envy the irresponsible life of the expedient communities we do well to remember that it sometimes has to be paid for by letting children die in order to adjust population

136

to food supply[1].

Any considerable freedom from natural limitations can be achieved only by suppressing spontaneity and accepting ideological limitations, and in the history of society the great advance came with acceptance of those belonging to the ideology of Principle, the ones that make reliance upon agriculture possible. The communities taking this step became able, in principle if not always in fact, to produce cattle and crops in the locations and the quantities they wished. Formerly limited to seldom much over fifty members, they were able to increase in size by a factor which one investigator sets at up to a thousand[2], and with size came power. Adjacent Expedient communities may sometimes impose reciprocal limitations upon each other, for example in the use of territory, but they can do little to restrain, or even to resist, the societies of Domination. The farming Bantu override their foraging neighbours and the Amazonian Indians are being decimated.

Whatever the first farmers may have expected we, looking back, can see that the new freedoms come accompanied by new burdens. As farming societies are relieved of the need to wander in search of food they become tied to their crops and herds; cultivation brought grinding labour of which the hunter-gatherers were happily ignorant. The advantages offered by farming and herding can be obtained only at the cost of adopting an ideology in which principles dominate impulses, an ideology requiring a firmly hierarchical social structure. Relative freedom from a substantial part of the limitations imposed by a raw external environment has been achieved at the cost of accepting ideological constraints.

We do not know the immediate occasion of the first transition and are not now likely to learn it. Material conditions, such as pressure of population or climatic change, are insufficient in themselves since they produce their effect only by way of ideology, contravening assumptions as to what the weather or the density of population ought to be. Whatever the reason, within a few thousand years after the first appearance of principle, domination, agriculture and sedentary society,

---

[1]Flood 1983, also Thomas 1959, 163
[2]Williams and Hunn 1986, 5

the population had increased enormously and expediency had been relegated to matters considered trivial, public and social affairs coming to be conducted by the new method of adherence to a set of principles. At least a large minority of people, many not themselves among those dominating society, came to prefer, in public affairs, the combination of freedoms and limitations offered by the new ideology to that of the original one. (The evidence for this is, of course, the spread of societies in which the new ideology overrode its predecessor).

With the organised regularity of the new society came writing and, later, printing. From this point on we have the record to refer to and it shows that, unlike the ideology of Expediency, that of Principle was not adopted by everybody. All societies of the new type maintain powerful and expensive institutions designed to discourage open contravention of established principles, demonstrating the continuing presence of a substantial group which has not internalised the new ideology. These institutions, however, are neither able nor intended to enforce compliance upon great numbers. As the ideology of Principle wins establishment it becomes one of the conditions to which the Expedient people find it convenient to adapt, with the result that coercion is needed only, as it were, to tidy up round the edges, restraining any tendency to backslide on the part of those adopting the new ideology and enforcing a degree of submission upon the few who persist in refusing even external compliance.

We also learn from the record that society moved on beyond the establishment of Principle. So long as any limitations persist the absolute assumption remains unsatisfied and the drive to overcome them continues. Most people confine their attention to the minor limitations constantly encountered in the practice of their current ideology, but some (without, of course, formulating their intentions in these terms) tackle the broader ones imposed by its more basic assumptions. They move on to a different ideology.

The universal rule, that limitations can be overcome only by accepting others, applies both to particular limitations and also to those sets of broad ones, influencing wide areas of behaviour, which seen from another angle appear as the sets of broad assumptions forming the main trunks of the major ideologies. One of these sets can be overcome only by assuming another set in its place, and since on each occasion the former limitations are overcome, not eliminated, the outcome is an increasingly complex dynamic system of sets of internalised limitations – which is to say assumptions – constituting the ideological structure.

The societies of Domination achieved their growing mastery over the natural world largely by shouldering the burden of that organised social activity we call work, something hardly known to the Expedient people, and they soon got themselves into a position where they no longer had much choice in the matter; if the vastly increased populations were to survive work had to continue. The need to work is very much a limitation, and the way to overcome it began to open with the advent of science and the technological advances that science makes possible: at first, machines to take the place of human or animal muscle and to overcome distance; later on, automation and computers. Ability to manipulate the environment and to move freely about in it, in short to overcome the limitations it imposes, took a giant leap forward, and the prospect of a leisurely life for all who wanted it began to open. Unlike the leisure of the first communities the new version rests upon a developed ability to manipulate large parts of the environment, but this requires acceptance of the limitations entailed in careful compliance with precise formulas. Those who would practice science, and endow society with the power that science makes possible, must go beyond getting things right in principle and subject themselves to a careful concern with the most minute of trifles; scientists habitually work to standards of accuracy greatly exceeding the capacity of their unaided senses, accepting limitations formerly unknown.

People not themselves scientists are also able to enjoy the new benefits, but only on condition that science continues to be practised. They come under an obligation to contribute towards its maintenance, and as it develops it grows more expensive; the cost of a particle accelerator is coming to exceed the resources of even the wealthiest nations; the next generation of equipment will require an international effort[1]. Once more, new freedoms come with new limitations.

Formerly a diversion for dilettantes, science has matured to become a working part of the social structure, and the new concern with accuracy sets the standards with which the more important social activities are required to comply. The society of Domination and Principle has become the society of self-limitation and Precision, accepting ideological restraints of a rigour its predecessor never knew. The state of its finances and the condition of its people are constantly monitored by the most exact methods that can be devised, its legal, educational and other systems undergo constant examination to keep them strictly in line with changing theories, its electoral systems operate by exact counting of individuals treated as identical units, and it possesses institutions, such as the National Council for Civil Liberties, and the many organisations working for various groups of the deprived, whose job it is to draw attention to abuses and malfunctions, striving to ensure that the society operates precisely as it ought. All of these are limitations the society imposes upon itself, and by accepting them it becomes so powerful that to act without self-restraint would be to risk destroying the environment (natural, social or both) and itself therewith. At this point social survival (that is to say freedom from extinction, the most severe of all limitations) comes to be inseparable from the type of political organisation I have termed the self-limiting state.

Disapproval of these developments and attempts to reverse them, both by private people and by governments, remain common, showing that many who accepted the ideology of Principle have held to it, not going on to precision. Precision does not eliminate principle but both completes and represses it, working to substitute for a condition in which things were right *only* in principle one in which they are *precisely* correct. Liberalism, the pursuit of precision in politics, does not try to do away with hierarchy but rather to validate it by matching it with human abilities, seeking to reduce the role played by hereditary rank, open privilege to meritocratic competition

---

[1] *Observer* newspaper, 20 November 1988

and make domination dependent upon achievement.

Possession of the new powers does not bring peace and plenty for all and the new freedom turns out to be far from complete. Benefits carry costs and there is no such thing as a free lunch; one set of limitations can be overcome only by accepting another. The states that provide the poorest of their citizens with facilities unimagined by Julius Caesar deprive them of the clean air the nomad takes for granted, wonder drugs produce side-effects and rapid transportation brings a higher body-count than many wars. The economy that delivers goods in profusion also produces unemployment, pollution, exhaustion of resources and destruction of needed food. Police have been known to misuse their powers and social workers sometimes harm the families they are paid to help. Medicine and public health measures extend the length of life that can be expected, perhaps the nearest thing to an absolute good that we can know, but this brings the threat of over-population, together with famine on a scale unknown to previous ages. Abounding wealth and grinding poverty exist side by side, the poor die younger than the rich, and over all hangs the new threat of nuclear extinction.

In their response to these things the adherents of Precision display the particulate mode of thought characteristic of their ideology. They tend strongly to take each difficulty by itself (they are sometimes known as "single-issue campaigners") and apply to it a particular treatment – a rearrangement of taxation, an agreement to forego the use of certain weapons, the substitution of small- for large-scale industry in the less developed countries. By such means as these the dangers are, usually and more or less, kept under control but only at the cost of maintaining the new arrangements, with all the burdens of restraint, expense, supervision, inspection and enforcement they entail.

The more acute of the difficulties suffered by the societies of Precision come for the most part from social rather than natural forces. At this point society largely replaces nature as the effective source of limitation, and accordingly the next development seeks to overcome social limitations. It uses the only method available, the acceptance of still more severe ideological ones. We all begin adult life inclined towards economic individualism and political collectivism; both these tendencies are subjected to increasing restraints through the stages of principle and precision, and with the advent of the next major ideology, that of Reform, restraint comes to be regarded as insufficient. Holding the difficulties encountered to be inevitable consequences of these inclinations it sets out to reverse them, substituting socialism for capitalism, co-operation for competition in economic affairs and freedom for control in political-intellectual matters.

Adherents of the reform ideology appeal for support on the ground that in a society of common ownership everybody will be better off, and not only in material things. The expected response has not been forthcoming; claiming to represent the majority interest, the members of this group remain a protesting minority, often winning minor victories but unable to establish their principles in the operation of society at large. They sometimes seek to escape from this position by allying themselves with a large eidostatic body (in Britain socialists join with the trade unions in the Labour Party) but the dog wags the tail not the tail the dog. A popular response to reformist proposals for a new society is that they may be all right in theory but will never work in practice, and whether the "never" be justified or not, the major ones at least have not yet worked even on a national scale; there has not been an egalitarian society with political freedom and common ownership of the means of production.

Instead of treating each difficulty on its merits, socialist reform relates them all to the principles on which society operates; these are held to be the root of all particular troubles, and substitution of their contraries the ultimate objective. The first method tried relies on the cumulative effect of many small and gentle changes to produce a major movement in the desired direction. After a century and more of reformist effort, however, it remains debatable whether any substantial progress towards the great goal has been achieved. In the advanced countries at least, living standards have improved for poor as well as rich but society remains obstinately hierarchical and authoritarian, and some of the worst things in human history have occurred while the reformist movement has been at work. With this ideology as with previous ones, most of its adherents retain their attachment, holding that the consequences of changing their gradualist approach for a fiercer one would be worse than those of holding to it. A minority, however, move on. Finding the limitations from which reformism suffers to be unacceptable they set out to overcome them by accepting a more rigorous ideology, one which restricts approved action to a narrower range but in doing so, they believe, renders that action more effective. They become revolutionaries. Communists work under the ideological restraint that they may not undertake reform for the sake of any benefits it may provide, but only as a contribution towards revolution. But communist revolution remains a mere aspiration so long as the great numbers retain their present ideologies, and they show no sign of substantial change. The revolutionaries remain even less numerous than the reformers and, consequently, even less influential.

The remaining one of the major ideologies introduced earlier sets out, as we will now expect, to overcome the limitations suffered by that of Revolution and to do so by accepting still more severe ideological limitations. All previous ideologies leave their adherents free to use the power of the state if they can. Even the communists, although envisaging a time when the state shall wither away, intend to use its power to reach that condition. The anarchist ideology forbids this, binding its adherents to repudiate authority even for themselves, and leadership too. It holds that the people cannot be dragooned, manoeuvred or even led into the free society but must achieve it for themselves, acting as autonomous individuals, and the purist anarcho-socialists of the Socialist Party of Great Britain carry this to the fine point of insisting that they must do so with conscious understanding of the reasons for their actions. The anarchist movement, in all its varieties, repudiates power, authority and leadership, and in doing so imposes upon itself the most severe ideological limitations of all. Apart from the occasional attempt at using force (negligible beside the violence routinely used by established governments) those who accept this ideology are not able to do more than attempt to spread it by theoretical discussion; any attempt at more directly practical or positive action falls short of, or contradicts, anarchist principles. (See, for example, Appendix A, Anarchism in Spain, p. 161).

From Expediency onward, progress along the range has meant acceptance of greater ideological restrictions in a dual sense. First, those immediately concerned accept assumptions prohibiting certain forms of behaviour. Second, they increasingly distance themselves from the great body of the people, who remain attached to the less sophisticated ideologies and, by virtue of their numbers, constitute the body and substance of society. Even now, even in the most highly-developed societies, the Expedient group is still larger than any other.

Each successive ideology is adopted by smaller numbers of people than the one before it, and used for a more restricted range of purposes. All who come to accept more sophisticated ideologies still conduct themselves for the most part Expediently, and those identified with precision continue to act, over a wide range, by Principle. With the best of intentions and the greatest of determination only a part of life can be conducted Precisely, and increasingly smaller parts by means of Reform, Revolution and Repudiation. In its fully-developed SPGB form Repudiation is used for practically nothing other than an attempt to spread the ideology of Repudiation.

Ideological development springs from the contradiction between the assumption of omnipotence (equally well seen as the absolute absence of all assumptions) and the limitations experienced as awareness grows of a world outside the self. Given this contradiction, and the intellectual potentialities of the human race, ideology results and moves through a series of stages, each of them repressing its predecessor. This succession cannot be simply pre-determined, for the details are largely arbitrary (almost any assumption can be formulated in a variety of ways) and the more general, less malleable assumptions cannot be sharply separated from the flexible particular ones. Each stage of development enables its successor rather than determining it, and had the world been different the ideological structure would doubtless be other than it is. Such issues verge on the philosophical; I put systematic ideology forward as a theory which extends our understanding of the society we have.

Readers who find that this chapter, more than others, fails to match up to the scope of its subject-matter, are in the right. I have been speaking about the interactions of six major ideologies within communities and societies which have been developing over very long periods, perhaps for millions of years. Each ideology, although capable of being conceptually reduced to a small number of highly general assumptions, functions in endlessly complex ways, and I have not attempted to do much more than trace one connecting thread through their inter-relationships. Physical science, after all, has not yet managed a general formula covering relationships between even three bodies.

The Evolution of Ideology

WE have distinguished three main stages of social development (four if one reckons the presence of the eidodynamics as constituting a distinct stage), each of them marked by the emergence of an ideological influence not previously active. We cannot precisely locate the first appearance of these influences and probably never shall be able to do so, for even animals, although mainly governed by genetic factors, do to some extent behave ideologically, making assumptions and choosing the expedient course; Walsby, a man who believed in doing a job thoroughly, traced the assumptive process back as far as the amoeba. Also, statements suggesting the presence of sophisticated modes of thought sometimes appear in the expedient communities. But here we are investigating the way societies work, and the major ideologies have not all been present, as significant social influences, since the beginnings of humanity. The ideological structure found today has come into being over time, and what has been said in the foregoing pages enables us to recognise its development as an evolutionary process. But let me emphasise at once that I do not suggest genetic transmission of ideology, or propose to make ideological transitions directly consequent upon biological developments.

Change usually attracts more attention than stability, and this has happened in the study of evolution, the biological world enjoying the limelight while its inanimate surroundings, for the most part less active, have been relegated to a supporting role. The term has become linked with the theory of natural selection and the name of Charles Darwin, and an orthodox view holds only genetic beings capable of true evolution. But natural selection was (I almost said "merely") Darwin's answer to the question: How does evolution operate in the biological world? The general concept arose much earlier. Charles' uncle Erasmus was familiar with it and the *Shorter Oxford Dictionary*, defining the word as "The process of evolving, unrolling, opening out or disengaging from an envelope" and adding that it is also used figuratively, dates its first appearance to 1647. I shall use "evolution" to mean the emergence of novelty out of a previous condition without extraneous addition, and in that sense it extends beyond the origination of species. The planetary, organic, human and social conditions evolved in that order, each arising from its predecessor without extraneous addition, and each of them serving as the base from which further novelty emerged. In this view genetic evolution becomes one stage in a process beginning with the elementary constituents of matter and embracing the whole of subsequent existence; substantial evolutionary advances have taken place in the absence of genes, and others in their presence but without their direct participation.

Evolution is often taken to be a smoothly continuous process, but the conception is over-simple. The importance of mutations in biological evolution has long been recognised, while laboratory work and the fossil record have both been providing increasing evidence of the part played by discontinuities. In evolution of the inorganic also – for example in the development of the stellar universe – sudden upheavals occur. I shall take evolution to be a process mainly continuous but, in whatever field it be studied, incorporating also those sporadic explosive releases of accumulated tensions that we term revolutions.

A healthy conceit tempts us to see evolution culminating in humanity, but to think in this way is to create an abstraction. Human beings are also animals and physical objects, and their continued existence depends upon the continuance of the organic and inorganic worlds. When we consider humanity in its context we see the concrete outcome of evolution to be the whole system of being, from inorganic matter to sophisticated society, and this can usefully be envisaged as a stepped pyramid, with each level resting upon the one below and each step upwards marked by the appearance of a complexity of organisation not formerly known. At the bottom lie the elementary constituents of matter and then, in ascending order, atoms, molecules, single cells, multi-cellular creatures, human beings, ideological groups and the societies they constitute.

There are, of course, significant differences between inorganic and organic evolution, and others between organic and ideological, one of these being that in ideological evolution acquired characteristics are transmitted (though not genetically). Each generation benefits from the experience of its predecessors, and one result of this has been that ideological evolution moves immensely faster than biological. Tens of millions of years from the amoeba to the first human beings, but a mere ten thousand from Expediency to Repudiation, with the latest steps taking only a century or two. The evolutionary *pattern*, however, the emergence of novelty without extraneous addition, leading to the development of a system of levels, each of them dependent upon its predecessor and exhibiting greater complexity of organisation, this persists from the inorganic through the organic and the human to the ideological and social.

Individual animals, races and species emerge and disappear, and so do particular sets of assumptions; my ideas of today differ from those I held yesterday, one theory displaces another, and even a relatively stable body like a main-sequence political party changes its policies and programmes from election to election, the discarded ones often never to be heard of again. But the broader evolutionary categories, the inorganic, the organic and the human, persist, and so do the major ideologies.

The single-celled creatures evolved in adaptation to a world without multi-cellular beings and are still capable of subsisting in such an environment, but the plants, fish, insects and animals, having evolved to fit a world of which single-celled life was a constituent, cannot long survive in its absence. Non-human life evolved in the absence of human beings and for the most part carries on happily without them, but they cannot survive without the animals and plants. Each of the broader evolutionary categories, having evolved in adaptation to an environment comprising its predecessor, depends upon the continuing presence of that forerunner for its own survival, and the rule holds good in ideological life. We found the ideology of Precision to have developed in adaptation to an environment comprising principle; remove this, so that precision comes face to face with un-Principled, un-Dominated Expediency, and it becomes unable to maintain itself. Liberalism, with its demand for political equality, can function only where coercive forces exist capable of suppressing disorder. Socialism, with its need for freedom of public speech in order to propagate its ideas, can survive only where liberalism, with its greater numbers and consequently stronger influence, is available to help maintain this freedom.

Reform depends upon Precision, Precision upon Principle and Principle upon the continuing presence of Expediency. Individual consumption, and living together in groups, both of them expressions of the expedient ethos, form the main foundation on which the activities of principle stand; without individual consumption, no social production; without gregariousness, no government. And the activities characteristic of the ideology of Precision similarly stand upon those of Principle: without social production, no science; without government, no power to correct malfunctions. This relationship of asymmetrical dependence (the later developments depending upon the earlier but not vice versa) continues throughout the series.

Adherents of the ideologies of Expediency, Principle and Precision tend to focus on the situation facing them, accepting, defending or improving society as it is and taking little interest in long-range theorising. It is mainly the eidodynamics who think about the course of future development, and they envisage society moving as a whole from one position to another; these advanced thinkers expect the general body of the people to assemble tomorrow where they themselves stand today, and the continuing absence of any such general advance is ascribed to malign influences which have to be eliminated. The eidodynamic movements set out, the more vigorously as they stand closer to that end of the range, to eliminate the economic individualism and political-intellectual compliance through which the eidostatic ideologies find expression and to succeed in that would be effectively to eliminate these ideologies. They set out to abolish, over a part of the universal system of evolution, the dependence of the later and more sophisticated developments upon the continuing functional presence of the earlier and simpler. Carried into biological evolution this approach would have human beings subsisting without food, air, or earth to stand on. Evolution certainly does include the emergence of successively more complex forms, but those who envisage it simply as an advance underestimate it, overlooking its integration of progress with stability. Most of the fundamental particles have not been taken up into living matter at all but continue to constitute the physical universe and by doing so make these higher developments possible.

In the absence of convincing evidence to the contrary the reasonable expectation has to be that the established pattern will persist, earlier developments serving as the enduring bases on which the later ones rest, and this is confirmed by recent political experience; even where eidodynamic movements have been in control of the state for generations they are finding themselves obliged to accept the eidostatic as constituting the bulk and substance of society. As they do this, in Russia and China for example, so the horrors resulting from the attempt to impose exclusively eidodynamic principles recede into history.

Once we cease taking society for granted, or thinking of it as a gift from God or an arbitrary creation of the human will, once we begin to recognise it as one term in the universal evolutionary process, we find ourselves virtually obliged to accept that each new phase in its development incorporates the functional relationships marking the previous condition. To treat any major ideology by itself is to create an abstraction; any given stage in ideological development comprises not just an ideology and the expression of it but also its context, with the previous ideologies in the series playing significant parts.

Taking this into account, the three main stages in the ideological development of society, which I have been calling (for reasons about to become obvious) simply...

- Expediency, Principle
- Domination and Precision
- self-limitation

... become...

- Expediency
- Expediency-with-Principle / Domination
- Expediency-with-Principle / Domination-and-Precision / self-limitation

... the fourth being...

- Expediency-with-Principle / Domination-and-Precision / self-limitation-and-the-eidodynamics

And if we wish to present an overall view we have to say that all life and all society consist of the elementary constituents of matter together with factors such as physiology, psychology and ideology which have emerged in the course of their increasingly complex organisation. (While saying this we need to remember that science has shown good reason for querying the materiality of these elementary constituents).[1]

As the later factors appear their development comes to form the cutting edge of evolution, the slower-moving changes of physical and biological beings receding into the background. Their various manifestations do not, however, interact directly, but always by a route which can be pictured as a descent from the higher to the lowest levels of organisation followed by a re-ascent. Revolutionaries can talk to each other only by submitting to the principles of grammar and making an expedient choice of words. Communication between ideological groups requires (to name only three of the main elements

---

[1] *Outline Sketch of Systematic Ideology* (p. 206) also discusses the range of the major ideologies. - publisher.

in a long and complex chain), psychology (the emotionally or aesthetically guided selection of a certain mode of speech or writing), physiology (internal processes which result in or constitute bodily movement) and physics (movement of material and fundamental particles, whether these be the constituents of air vibrating to form sound waves, the constituents of ink and paper, or the electronic events which produce effects upon computer screens). Communication, essential for performance of the activities which distinguish the higher evolutionary levels, depends upon the continuing presence of the lower.

In thinking about evolution attention tends to focus on the differing qualities exhibited by the various levels, but the system also exhibits regular quantitative relationships. There are fewer atoms than fundamental particles, fewer molecules than atoms, fewer cells than molecules, fewer multi-cellular beings than cells, fewer human beings than multi-cellular creatures, fewer ideological groups then human beings, fewer societies than ideological groups[1]. The higher the level of organisation the lower the number of units to be found on it[2].

It is seldom possible to count such units, but the absolute number on each level is usually irrelevant; nearly always only relative magnitudes matter, and the disproportion between the numbers on the different levels tends to be self-evident. The major barrier to understanding an evolutionary system usually lies in the difficulty of discriminating between, on the one hand, the features which mark off one type of unit from another on the same level and, on the other, those which distinguish the units on one level from those on the adjoining ones; once this has been accomplished the significant quantitative relationships usually leap to the eye.

The relationship between level of development and numerosity holds good within the ideological structure. If we construct a diagram in which the vertical dimension represents

---

[1] To the extent that societies remain independent of each other the ideological groups of each have also to be reckoned as independent of those of the others. Only if "society" be taken to mean one world-wide organisation can we reckon just one major ideological group on each level.

[2] In thinking about levels of ideological development it needs to be borne in mind that a high death rate is seldom taken as a good thing and when we call a statement the height of absurdity this does not mean we think particularly well of it. "Higher" is not a synonym for "better."

degree of ideological development, and horizontal extension the relative magnitude of the group at each stage, we get the stepped figure known in systematic ideology as the ideological pyramid (p. 177), and from what has been said in this chapter we recognise this as the uppermost part of a far larger pyramid incorporating also the pre-ideological levels of biological activity, with inorganic matter spreading out below those and the fundamental particles forming the base.

Conclusion

IN the opening pages I noted that a theory of ideology must account for the presence of differing ideologies within the one society. Systematic ideology explains the major or main-sequence ideologies as stages in the universal system of evolution and the minor ideologies, the more localised and transient ones, as specialised versions of one or another of these. No part of the evolutionary system is static; the major ideologies have not always existed as they are and we have to expect them to continue changing in future. But in ideology as elsewhere change moves at varying speeds, the category outlasting its individual constituents and the general enduring while particulars perish. Although the detailed ideas of the modern city-dweller have little in common with those of the early forager, the largest ideological group within our mechanised, computerised, automated, nuclear-powered, space-traveling civilisation retains substantially the ethos and the set of general assumptions by which the first human communities operated.

We must resist the temptation to draw any rigid distinction between fluctuating particular assumptions and unchanging general ones, for when the particulars change the general which they constitute cannot remain entirely unaffected. But one brick may crumble without seriously affecting the proposition that bricks are hard, solid things suitable for building houses, and a change in one particular may have its effect largely canceled by contrary changes in others; as some people die others get born and the human race goes on. The highly general assumptions forming the bases of the major ideologies change so slowly that when studying their influence upon human societies (rather than seeking eternal verities) they are best regarded as stable. Systematic ideology deals for the most part with enduring regularities; usually harder to discern than transient local disturbances, and often less dramatic, these are not therefore less worthy of study.

The major ideologies form a system, that is to say a structure in dynamic equilibrium, its parts interdependent and

154

a change in one tending to produce compensatory effects in others. People trying to bring about social changes tend to work on the assumption that other things will stay as they are, and the limited validity of this accounts for much of the disappointment they so often suffer. Each change in the tax laws brings a fresh crop of devices for avoiding taxation, and the French leaders of 1789 did not have to contend with anything corresponding to the powerful, cohesive, widespread and deep-rooted conservative organisations of today; it was their own success that called these forth to hinder later revolutionaries[1]. Many attempts at change are absorbed without noticeable effect, while those that achieve a measure of success alter not only the abuse or malfunction aimed at but also other parts of the system with which it interacts. Being diffused their effect is usually less than their proponents hope and, touching on features these did not take into account, often different from what they expect. Instead of building up momentum the changes intended as steps towards socialism, communism or anarchism tend to be countered by reverse swings and backlashes.

Ideological behaviour, whether in politics or elsewhere, is purposeful by definition, but when multiple purposes interact the outcome is often something intended by none of the participants. The French revolutionaries did not intend the rule of Napoleon, the Chinese the events in Tiananmen Square, the original Bolsheviks the horrors of Stalinism or the English anti-monarchists the domination of Cromwell. The Weimar Republic did not intend to prepare the way for Hitler and neither the Bolsheviks nor the Nazis nor the scientists who first "split the atom" intended a confrontation between two nuclear superpowers. Turning from great things to lesser, the electors who repeatedly voted Labour governments, with their socialist connections, into office, did not intend that these should be followed by a succession of administrations more vigorously and directly anti-socialist than any previously known in Britain. Although not static the ideological system is so integrated as to be self-adjusting, self-correcting, self-

---

[1] O'Sullivan 1976, 9

stabilising, and it tends towards a condition in which the influence exercised by each major ideology diminishes as it stands closer to the anarchist end of the range. There is nothing mystical about this; it has come about in the course of evolutionary development within a natural environment at best neutral and sometimes, in effect though without intention, actively hostile. If there were any societies which set out on a different course they have not survived.

In their search for dramatic headlines the media focus upon failure and disaster, but the worst problems immediately facing us arise from uncontrolled success. Acting as economic individualists, each person and each group pursuing their own perceived interests without regard for the effects upon the total human community, the eidostatics have brought society to a point where it possesses powers capable of providing for all its members with a profusion never known before. Those same powers also make it possible for even single firms to do significant damage to the environment, and for individual nations to destroy civilisation, perhaps to put an end to the human race. The eidodynamics seek, with greater single-mindedness as they are more extreme, to end these threats by doing away with (what they believe to be) the cause of them; they propose a society which shall suppress economic individualism and function by economic collectivism alone. They want to cut off the branch they are sitting on. They have not succeeded and do not seem likely to do so; the methods they advocate, even when tried, have not been widely taken up. Proudhon's workshops and the communities founded by Fourier, Saint Simon and Robert Owen have faded away, Soviet Russia and People's China are returning to a reliance upon competition and profit, and the socialistic *kibbutzim* are no longer seen as the flower of Israel. The eidodynamics can validly claim that the persistent adherence of the great numbers to the old familiar ways has frustrated them, but it was just that attachment they set out to overcome. To say that if the people had supported them they would have succeeded is like saying that if we all had wings there would be no road accidents; doubtless true, but not helpful.

The impression given by the above paragraphs, that the eidodynamics have so far failed, comes from judging them by their own standard; they have indeed made little progress towards a society operating exclusively, or even predominantly, by the principles of socialism, communism or anarchism; their effectiveness has lain in another direction. My earlier statement, that the eidostatics have brought this society close to the point where it becomes able to provide abundantly for all its members, was one-sided and incomplete. This has been achieved by our total society, with the eidodynamic parties and movements among its working parts. Not only the accepters, supporters and improvers of existing society but also its critics, opponents and would-be destroyers, the Diggers, the Communards, Babeuf, Karl Marx, Bakunin, the Chicago anarchists, Mao and his comrades of the Long March, the Bolsheviks and Mensheviks, Trotsky and the socialists working inside the Labour Party, the Spanish POUM and the SPGB, all of these have helped to make it what it is. The effects they produced were sometimes direct, sometimes indirect, sometimes the contrary of what they intended. Some of the results of eidodynamic efforts can be traced in education, in ways of treating the sick and the insane, in attitudes towards immigrants, in restraints upon weapons and the use of war as an instrument of policy. Other results of their work may be harder to see but more pervasive, atmospheres or influences. Whenever the eidodynamics produced any effect at all they contributed towards our present condition. Before dismissing this as yet more evidence of their failure, let us remember that in spite of all the wars, famines and disasters the population continues to increase. The nearest thing we have to an absolute standard by which to judge a society is its ability to maintain human life, and now people are flourishing as never before. So much so that the freedom of individuals to reproduce will probably have to be restrained, for the sake of the whole community. A consequence mainly of improved medicine, sanitation and food-production, this is not failure but rather an overabundance of success; human abilities are coming to exceed the capacity of the planet. Pollution, damage to the environment, and the dangers that come with nuclear energy, from poisoning of workers in the industry to the threat of universal extinction, are all of them consequences of our increased power over the environment. Power is always dangerous, but so far humanity has benefited from it, and the eidodynamic insistence that the welfare of the total community must take precedence over the interests of individuals, whether these be people, firms, industries or nations, has had much to do with this. It may well be due to their efforts, especially since 1945, that we are still here at all. The eidodynamics have been playing their part in an undertaking which has created our present problems by succeeding beyond all expectation. If they choose to turn away from the achievement, dressing in sackcloth and ashes for their failure to set up socialism, communism or anarchism, well, that is a luxury they have earned. What might have happened without them we can never know. What *has* happened, the astonishing success that we have not yet learnt how to handle, has come about partly as a result of their efforts.

In the material-economic field the eidostatic with its demand for freedom of activity provides the driving force and the eidodynamic, with its insistence on the need for control, the stabilising restraint, while in political-intellectual matters this is reversed. We have seen something of the systematic relationships which closer examination reveals between the ideologies which constitute these classes. The arrangement leaves no ideology without its function and no social activity unaccounted for, and such neatness arouses suspicion, but this weakens when we recall that we are dealing not merely with correspondence but identity. To a large extent the society *is* the ideological structure, expressed as institutions and activities, and the ideological structure *is* the society (and the world), internalised as a system of sets of assumptions.

In speaking of relationships between ideologies, ideological classes and ideological groups I have not been proposing a new system which could work if only people would think and behave differently, but presenting an interpretation of what has happened in the past and is happening now. Projection into the future of the course followed to this point does not suggest that society has reached its final condition, but it does affect ideas about the changes that can reasonably be expected. Proposals requiring virtual elimination of the less sophisticated ideologies, or their reduction to impotence, are not likely to be any more successful in future than they have been in the past.

Everything real has at least two sides. This applies to social systems as well as material objects, and appreciation of the benefits brought by industrial society confirms the eidostatic stance, while recognition of the troubles and dangers it creates reinforces the tendency of the eidodynamics to seek radical changes. Insulated by the social structure from some of the greater natural limitations (a condition they sometimes express by saying the problem of production has been solved), the eidodynamics strive to overcome the limitations their society imposes but find themselves frustrated by lack of support. In moving through the successive eidodynamic stages this comes to be seen as the deepest problem facing them. Socialists treat it as little more than a result of inadvertence, something to be cured readily enough if only they could obtain control of the educational system and the means of mass communication. Communism ascribes it to the influence of the capitalist class and prescribes a proletarian dictatorship as the cure. Anarchism rejects this, pointing to the continuing suppression of political freedoms where the capitalists have been expropriated; it maintains that the liberated society can only come as a result of the free movement of the people themselves. At the eidodynamic extreme the SPGB add that for such an effort to be successful it must be undertaken by a majority which understands and accepts their account of the structure and operation of society. The people who work for a living, they say, run society "from top to bottom," operating not only the productive and distributive systems but also the schools, universities, banks, stock exchanges, newspapers, radio and television stations, police forces, armies and bureaucracies. On this analysis it has to be agreed that if the overwhelming majority of these people were to decide to brush the authorities aside and set up the liberated society for themselves nothing could stop them. The conception leaves only one question unanswered: Why does the general body of the people not accept these proposals?

Systematic ideology provides an answer, as yet only in general terms, and needing far more development, but supported by reason and evidence and opening the way to a new understanding of social development past and future. The undertaking has required an activity covered by none of the ideologies we have been discussing, namely the study of ideology conceived as one constituent of universal evolution. With this our work comes full circle, the theory of systematic ideology accounts for itself. The ideology underlying this book has to be added to the range. Lying beyond the eidodynamic it has evolved in the same way as the other major ideologies. That evolution, however, is far from having followed a smoothly continuous course, and the emergence of this further term in the series results from yet another revolution in thinking. For ideology to be understood in this way it has to be accepted as a relatively independent field, intimately related to other social activities (and, beyond these, to the biological and physical worlds) but not reducible to them without loss of the features that make it what it is. If we are to understand ideology and its consequences, the tendency to treat the major ideologies as secondary effects produced by the social structure, or some part of it such as class interests, has to be conceptually repressed. Rather is the social structure with its classes a consequence of ideology.

The question arises whether further major ideologies have yet to appear. It seems unlikely, for with the appearance of the ideology which has for its particular function the study of ideology the series turns back on itself. Does this mean that ideological evolution is finished? I know of no reason to think so. There are no perceptible limits to the growth of knowledge or the extension of understanding, and new versions of the major ideologies, new ideological species as it were, continue to appear. One recent instance was fascism, clearly cognate with Domination yet possessing features peculiar to itself. I have spoken above of the greens, a new eidodynamic construction, and many readers will have felt that other parties, tendencies or organisations should have been taken into account. More political movements than it is well possible to list struggle for a place on the stage, and party politics is only a small part of ideological activity. New sciences appear, new religions and new mysticisms, new theories, new professions, new trades, new psychologies and new entertainments, each of them an ideological development. More than ever before, our world is a boiling, bounding, bubbling ferment of ideological novelty, and the rate of change is accelerating. If the ideological system has reached completion it is only in the sense that a newborn child is complete.

Appendix A: Anarchism in Spain

ONE apparent exception to the rule, that the nearer to anarchism a movement stands the smaller and weaker it tends to be, is provided by the strength of the anarchist movement in Spain prior to and during the Civil War. In discussing this I rely mainly on *The Spanish Civil War* by Hugh Thomas and *The Spanish Anarchists; the heroic years 1868-1936* by Murray Bookchin. Thomas writes as a detached scholar, Bookchin as an enthusiast for Spanish anarchism; neither intends to support the conclusion I draw from their work.

Spanish anarchism was divided between the large trade union organisation, the CNT (translating, roughly, as National Confederation of Labour), and the much smaller FAI (Iberian Anarchist Federation). Thomas says that in Barcelona in 1936 there were 350,000 anarchists; that over a million and a half Spanish workers were anarchists in outlook in the 30s, that in June 1931 the anarchists claimed 600,000 members, 250,000 of them in Catalonia. He quotes Balcells as saying the CNT had 58 per cent of the workers in Barcelona and between thirty per cent and thirty-five per cent of those in Catalonia, and Peirat as saying the FAI was 30,000 strong in 1936[1]. Bookchin claim about a million members for the CNT in 1935[2]. Bearing in mind that the population of Spain in 1936 was only twenty-four million, the anarchist movement there was, as Bookchin says, immense; far greater than systematic ideology would lead us to expect.

The discrepancy largely disappears when we realise that the Spanish "anarchists" thought and behaved differently from the movements known by that title elsewhere. This appears in many ways. Bookchin speaks of the FAI convening assemblies "to allow for a full expression of rank and file views," and neither the distinction, between rank and file members and others, nor the implied possibility, that full expression of views might not be allowed, is to be found in anarchist movements

---

[1]Thomas 1977, 69,70
[2]Bookchin 1977, 1

162

outside Spain. "... dissidents were permitted a considerable degree of freedom in voicing and publishing material against the leadership and established policies." Freedom *permitted*? And *leadership*? Among anarchists? This is no verbal slip on Bookchin's part; in the preceding paragraph, also, these anarchists are said to have had leaders, and "very aggressive" ones at that[1].

If there is one single feature which identifies anarchists (as that term is used in anarchist movements outside Spain and in systematic ideology) it is the repudiation, among themselves as elsewhere, of authority and leadership. The Spaniards behaved differently, Bookchin saying of the FAI: "It had been led by its centrist members into shadowy violations of anarchist principle[2]." That "shadowy" would be better replaced by "gross."

Thomas confirms: "The FAI leader, Abad de Santillan," "the political leaders of the Anarchists," "nearly two million workers... organised in the CNT and directed by a secret society, the FAI," "The CNT, which was from the start dominated by Anarchists," the FAI "a revolutionary elite dedicated to lead the masses... " "the FAI's aspirations to elite leadership," "the leaders of the Seville Anarchists," "the Anarchist leadership," "Federica Montseney the Anarchist leader[3]."

Thomas makes it clear that the presence of leadership and authority within the Spanish movement of which he writes is not a misconception that he, not himself (as far as I know) an anarchist, has introduced: "On 27 September the Anarchists, having held the reality of authority" [!!!] "in Barcelona since the rising, accepted it formally by entering the Generalidad" [the governing body of Barcelona]. This was "the first entry of an Anarchist movement into a position of political authority," but it was not to be the last. A month later four anarchist leaders became Ministers in the Madrid government, and not as isolated or eccentric individuals. They "had previously been elected as the appropriate members of their organisation [the CNT] to join the government at a 'plenum' of the move-

---

[1]Bookchin 1977, 214
[2]*ibid* 223
[3]Thomas 1977, 528,657,6,65,68,73,119,277,277

ment." One of these four "anarchist" rulers became Minister of Justice. As Thomas remarks, "libertarian Anarchists of the past would have turned in their graves." He has earlier sumarised Bakunin's views on these matters:

> All collaboration with parliaments, governments and organised religion was to be condemned. Criminals would be punished by the censure of public opinion[1].

Perhaps I am labouring the point beyond reason. It is, after all, clear enough that people who fight and kill and die in defence of a government, heroic as they may be, are not acting like anarchists in any normal sense of the term.

---

[1]Thomas 1977, 471, 538, 60

Appendix B: The Absolute Assumption

THE absolute assumption being the assumption of an unlimited, indeterminate condition remains totally undefined; it may equally well be seen as the absence of any assumptions. In taking off from an indefinite base Walsby's system is at one with psychoanalysis and Pavlovian reflexology and, beyond these, with two systems of thought even more authoritative and widely respected, namely physical science and the theory of biological evolution. None of these starts, as his does, from an explicit absence of definition, but each of them builds on a foundation innocent of the precise demarcations that play so large a part in formal logic, an approach which does much to account for their great scope. No system can account for features taken for granted to get it started; the more indefinite the original condition the more comprehensive the capacity of the system. At the root of Pavlov's system lies the inborn, unconditioned tendency to make purposeless movements that he termed "the freedom reflex." In the Freudian view of personal development the id, an incoherent tumult of desire, forms the basis. Biological evolution begins with the single-celled creature, not bound into any organisation and often indefinite in shape, and physical science finds its base in the fundamental particles of matter, neither material nor immaterial (or both at once), and subject to the principle of uncertainty. (While speaking of beginnings we can add Genesis I.2: "And the earth was without form, and void... ").

The absolute assumption, the first one to be made, constitutes the undetermined base of the eventual ideological structure, prohibiting interpretation of ideological behaviour entirely in terms of external influences; the assumption of absolute freedom is the one content of the ideology that does not reach it via the senses. It comes to be repressed, but never abandoned, and tension originating in the discrepancy between this assumption and the result of any attempt to externalise (realise) it provides the motivation of ideological development.

Select Bibliography

Auden, W. H. and Kronenberger L. (eds.) 1964. *The Faber Book of Aphorisms.* London: Faber and Faber.

Banton M. (ed.) 1966. *The Anthropology of Complex Societies.* London: Tavistock Publications.

Barclay H. 1982. *People Without Government.* London: Kahn and Averill with Cienfuegos Press.

Barrett D. B. 1982. *The World Christian Encyclopedia; A comparative study of churches and religions in the modern world AD 1900-2000.* Nairobi, Oxford, NY: OUP.

Benn, Tony 1982. *Arguments for Democracy.* Harmondsworth: Penguin Books.

Bentley M. 1987. *The Climax of Liberal Politics; British liberalism in theory and practice 1868-1918.* London: Edward Arnold.

Billig M. 1978. *Fascists; a social psychological view of the National Front.* London and New York: Harcourt Brace Jovanovitch.

Black, Bob. Undated, but after 1985. *The Abolition of Work and Other Essays.* Port Townsend: Loompanics Unlimited.

Boas F. 1911. *The Mind of Primitive Man.* New York. MacMillan and Co.

Bookchin, Murray. 1977. *The Spanish Anarchists; the heroic years 1868-1936.* New York: Free Life Editions.

Brand C. F. 1965. *The British Labour Party, a short history.* Stanford, Calif: Stanford U.P., Oxford U.P.

Brody H. 1988. *Living Arctic; Hunters of the Canadian North.* London: Faber and Faber.

Bullock A. and Shock M. (eds.) 1967. *The Liberal Tradition from Fox to Keynes.* Oxford: Clarendon Press.

Burnford S. 1974. *One Woman's Arctic.* London: New English Library.

Burrow J. W. 1981. *A Liberal Descent; Victorian historians and the English past.* Cambridge: Cambridge University Press.

Carver T. 1989 *Friedrich Engels, his life and thought.* London: MacMillan.

Checkland S. G. 1971. *The Gladstones, a family biography 1764-1851.* Cambridge: Cambridge University Press.

Childe V. G. 1936. *Man Makes Himself.* London: Watts and Co.

Clark G. 1983. *Mesolithic Prelude.*

Cobban A. 1956 "The Vocabulary of Social History"; in *Political Science Quarterly,* Volume XXXI (March 1956).

Cohen J. M. and M.J. eds. *The Penguin Dictionary of Quotations.* Penguin Books 1960

Dawkins R. 1976. *The Selfish Gene.* Oxford: Oxford University Press.

Doolittle I. G. 1982. *The City of London and Its Livery Companies.* Dorchester: Gavin Press.

Doyle M. W. 1986. *Empires.* Ithaca and London: Cornell Biniversity Press.

Durkheim E. 1947. *The Division of Labour in Society.* Glencoe, Illinois.

Ellen, R. 1982. *Environment, subsistence and system. The ecology of small-scale social formations.* Cambridge: Cambridge University Press.

Evans-Pritchard E. E. 1962. *Essays in Social Anthropology.* London: Faber and Faber.

— 1951. *Kinship and Marriage Among the Nuer.* Oxford: Clarendon Press.

— 1950. *The Nuer; a description of the modes of livelihood and political institutions of a Nilotic people.* Oxford: Clarendon Press.

Finley M .I. 1958. *Ancient History, Evidence and Models.* London: Chatto and Windus.

Flood J. 1983. *Archaeology of the Dreamtime.* Sydney and London: Wm. Collins Ltd.

Freuchen P. 1962. *Book of the Eskimos.* London: Arthur Barker Ltd.

Gellner E. 1988. *Plough, Sword and Book; the structure of human history.* London: Collins Harvill.

Gilmour I. 1977. *Inside Right; a study of Conservatism.* London: Hutchinson.

Gouldner A.W. 1985. *Against Fragmentation; the origins of Marxism and the sociology of intellectuals.* Oxford: Oxford University Press.

Guérin D. 1970. *Anarchism from Theory to Practice.* Trans. Klopper. New York and London: Monthly Review Press.

Hilliard W. H. 1968. *The People in Between; the Pitjanjatjara people of Ernabella.* London: Hodder and Stoughton.

Hinton W. 1983. *Fanshen; a documentary of revolution in a Chinese village.* London: Martin Secker and Warburg.

Horton R, and Finnegan R. Eds. 1973. *Modes of Thought; essays in thinking in western and non-western societies.* London: Faber and Faber.[1]

Humphrey C. 1983. *Karl Marx Collective; economy, society and religion in a Siberian collective farm.* Cambridge: Cambridge University Press.

Jacobs J. 1970 *The Economy of Cities.* London: Jonathan Cape.

Keegan J. 1977. *The Face of Battle.* London: Jonathan Cape.

Keegan J. and Holmes R. 1985. *Soldiers; a history of men in battle.* London: Hamish Hamilton.

Konner M. 1982. *The Tangled Wing; biological constraints on the human spirit.* London: Heinemann.

Kuhn T. S. 1975. *The Structure of Scientific Revolutions.* University of Chicago Press.

Kuper L. 1982. *Genocide, its Political Use in the Twentieth Century.* New Haven and London: Yale University Press.

Lamm Z. 1984. "Ideologies in a Hierarchical Order: a neglected theory."; In *Science and Public Policy,* February 1984.

Lawick-Goodall J.van. 1974. *In the Shadow of Man.* Glasgow: Fontana Books.

Leacock E. and Lee R. 1982. *Politics and History in Band Societies.* Cambridge: Cambridge University Press.

Lenin 1973. *What is to be Done?* Peking: Foreign Languages Press.

— 1964. "Imperialism, the Highest Stage of Capitalism"; in *Collected Works.* (Mommsen, p. 47)

Levi-Strauss C. 1966. *The Savage Mind.* London: Weidenfeld and Nicholson.

Lowie R. H. 1937. *The History of Ethnological Theory.* London: George R.Harrap and Co.

---

[1] ¶X

Manuel F. E. 1973. *The Religion of Isaac Newton; (the Fremantle Lectures)*. Oxford: Clarendon Press (1974).

Manuel F. E. and F. P. 1979. *Utopian Thought in the Western World*. Oxford: Basil Blackwell.

Marx K. and Engels F. 1978. *Manifesto of the Communist Party*; in Feuer L.S. (ed.) *Karl Marx and Friedrich Engels, Basic Writings on Politics and Philosophy*. London: Collins, Fontana Books.

— 1970. *The German Ideology Part One*. London: Lawrence and Wishart.

Mill J. S. n.d. *On Liberty*. Chicago and New York: Belford, Clarke and Co.

Milligan S. 1987. Quoted in *Sunday Times* newspaper 5 July.

Mitchell A. 1990. *A Fragile Paradise: nature and man in the Pacific*. London: Collins.

Mithen S. J. "To Hunt or to Paint: Animals and Art in the Upper Palaeolithic"; in *MAN, the Journal of the Royal Anthropological Institute*, Volume 23 No.4, December 1988.

Mommsen W. J. 1981. *Theories of Imperialism*. London: Weidenfeld and Nicholson.

Morris J. 1981. *Farewell the Trumpets*. Harmondsworth: Penguin Books.

Morris J. 1980. *Heaven's Command*. Harmondsworth: Penguin Books.

Naess A. and Associates. 1956. *Democracy, Ideology and Objectivity*. Oxford: Basil Blackwell.

Newman, John Henry 1986. *Loss and Gain*. Oxford: Oxford University Press.

O'Grady J. 1985. *Heresy; heretical truth or orthodox error?* Shaftesbury: Element Books.

O'Sullivan N. 1976. *Conservatism*. London: J.M.Dent and Sons Ltd.

Parsons T. 1977. *The Evolution of Societies*. Toby ed. Englewood Cliffs, New Jersey: Prentice-Hall.

Pêcheux M. 1983. *Language, Semantics and Ideology*. Harbans Nagpal trans. London: MacMillan.

Popper K. R. 1952-45. *The Open Society and its Enemies*. London: Volume 1 Routledge and Kegan Paul 1952; Volume 2 George Routledge and Sons Ltd. 1945.

Ralph P. L. 1973. *The Renaissance in Perspective*. London: G.Bell and Sons.

Richards V. (ed.) 1987. *Why Work? arguments for the leisure society*. London: Freedom Press.

Roberts D. 1988. *The Penguin Dictionary of Politics*. Harmondsworth: Penguin Books.

Robson G. C. 1928. *The Species Problem*. Edinburgh: Oliver and Boyd.

Rose R. 1974. *The Problem of Party Government*. Harmondsworth: Penguin Books.

Sagan C. 1985. *At the Dawn of Tyranny; the origins of individualism, political oppression and the state*. New York: Alfred A.Knopf.

Sahlins M. 1988. *Stone Age Economics*. London and NY. Routledge.

Samizdat, November 1988. London.

Service E. R. 1966. *The Hunters*. New Jersey: Prentice-Hall Inc.

— 1975. *Origins of the State and Civilization; the process of cultural evolution*. New York: W. W. Norton and Company Inc.

Socialist Party of Great Britain 1904. *Our Object and Declaration of Principles*. London: Socialist Party of Great Britain.

— 1969. *Questions of the Day*. London: Socialist Party of Great Britain.

— 1986. *Women and Socialism*. London: Socialist Party of Great Britain.

Stevenson, Robert F. 1968. *Population and Political Systems in Tropical Africa*. New York: Columbia University Press.

Thomas E. M. 1959. *The Harmless People*. London: Seeker and Warburg.

Thomas, Hugh. 1977. *The Spanish Civil War*. Harmondsworth: Penguin Books.

Thompson, John B., 1984 *Studies in the Theory of Ideology*. Cambridge and Oxford: Polity Press and Basil Blackwell.

Treglown J. In *Times Literary Supplement* 19 May 1989.

Trotter W. 1940. *Instincts of the Herd in Peace and War*. London: Ernest Benn Ltd.

Turnbull C. 1984. *The Forest People*. London: Granada Publishing Ltd.

Walsby, Harold. 1947. *The Domain of Ideologies. a study of the origin, development and structure of ideologies*. Glasgow: Wm. McLellan in Collaboration with the Social Science Association.

— n.d.(c.196-?) *History of the Dialectic*. (Unpublished paper).

Warren B. 1980. *Imperialism, Pioneer of Capitalism*. Sender ed. London: Verso.

Westfall R. S. 1980. *Never at Rest, a biography of Sir Isaac Newton*. Cambridge: Cambridge University Press.

Whitehorn K. 1987. In the *Observer* newspaper 19 April.

Williams N. M. and Hunn E.S. eds. 1986. *Resource Managers; North American and Australian hunter-gatherers*. A.C.T.: Australian Institute of Aboriginal Affairs.

Woodcock G. 1963. *Anarchism; a history of libertarian ideas and movements* Harmondsworth: Penguin Books.

Synopsis

SYSTEMATIC Ideology - A study of the Structure, origin and evolution of ideologies.

Introduction

Ideology, usually seen as a distorting influence, is best understood as a normal part of social life. Karl Marx's class theory of ideology is the only one to win much acceptance; further experience since his time has shown that it accounts only for some of the minor ideologies, not the major ones we shall be studying. Social development has not followed the course expected by the socialists and communists and in seeking the reason for this we discover the fundamental importance of ideology.

The Political Series

We start where ideology is most familiar; in politics. The main-sequence political movements in Britain are distinguished by the general ideas they respectively hold. When arranged in a certain order they form a significant series, ideas which are small and weak in the movement standing at one extreme growing bigger and stronger in moving along the range. As these ideas develop so the successive movements become smaller and less influential. The same series, under different names but exhibiting substantially the same features, appears throughout the advanced world, and it includes the very large group of non-political people as one of its terms.

From Politics to Ideology

The general ideas held by the different movements occur in definite sets, all those who support each movement holding the same set; this constitutes them a group and distinguishes that group from others. These sets of ideas govern political behaviour but operate mainly below the level of awareness, people rarely knowing clearly what their own set comprises. This means they are best termed not "general ideas" but assumptions. The sets have become known as the ideologies of the movements, but it is not only in politics that the set of assumptions, the ideology, governs behaviour. It does so every time we act with purpose, in whatever field. Each of the major ideologies is linked with a distinct pattern of behaviour, an ethos; this more readily recognisable than the underlying set of assumptions, and providing a descriptive name for the ideology, one which does not imply limitation to political matters.

Ideology Beyond Politics

We all enter adult life with the same ideology. Some people go on to develop another. In doing this they repress but do not eliminate the original one; it continues to influence their behaviour although in ways they consider unimportant. Some of these go on to develop a third ideology, some of those yet another, and so on, the previous ideology being retained in each case and continuing to influence behaviour although under repression. The primal ideology, that of the non-political people, inclines its adherents rather away from work than towards it. Each ideology beyond that inclines its adherents towards a particular complex of activities, one complex including government, agriculture, traditional education, production and institutional religion, another including the hard sciences, accountancy, logic and nonconformist religion.

The Beginnings

The major ideologies have emerged in the course of social development. For much the greater part of the time humanity has existed the only mode of life was that of the hunter-gatherers, and this expressed the primal ideology. As their title implies, these people did not produce their own food. In their communities work (in the sense of a joint productive enterprise) was unknown, and they did not have government either.

From Village to Empire

Government and agriculture (entailing work) appeared together some 10,000 years ago, and the other members of the complex of activities associated with the second ideology quickly followed. This ideology accounts for social development from the first appearance of institutionalised control (by "big men" and chieftains) to the great empires of recent times.

After the Empires

The next major ideology, after preliminary appearances in the English Civil War and elsewhere, became established as a social influence with the French Revolution. It is responsible for the movements which led the colonies to throw off imperial rule and for the transition (not yet complete) from imperialism to a world-wide system of independent states each respecting the independence of the others. The communities living by the first ideology gathered their food; those of the second lived by agriculture and herding, using human and animal muscle-power; the next ideology brought science, with machinery and science-based industry.

The Eidodynamics

The remaining ideologies in the series (roughly speaking, those which appear in politics as socialism, communism and anarchism) have not succeeded in establishing forms of society which express their principles; they remain influences and aspirations. These movements expect the general body of the people to adopt the ideologies favoured by the reformers and revolutionaries in place of those they now hold, but there are no good grounds for this expectation. Confirmation of this is found in comparison of the pattern followed by social development with that of progress in science, as presented in Kuhn's *Structure of Scientific Revolutions*.

The Origins of Ideologies

Purposeful action has to be adapted to the circumstances but we never know in full detail and with complete certainty what these may be. We are obliged to make assumptions and then to adapt our behaviour to circumstances as we assume them to be. This is why different groups living under the one set of social conditions behave differently; they are making different assumptions. By explaining how the principal sets of assumptions, the major ideologies, arise, systematic ideology helps us to understand why the main social groups behave as they do.

The Evolution of Ideology

The major ideologies emerge as results of a non-genetic evolutionary process, each of them forming part of the environment to which its successor is adapted and its continued existence therefore being needed for the continued existence of that successor. This is why all the earlier major ideologies including the primal one, that of the hunter-gatherers, persist today as working parts of our social structure. Each major ideology depends upon its predecessor, the primal ideology depends upon the living animal and that in turn upon the inorganic world. Ideology is a continuation of the system of universal evolution which began with the fundamental particles of matter.

Conclusion

The alarmists would have us believe that we stand on the brink of disaster. If they are right, this is not the result of failure; our worst problems arise from uncontrolled success. In order to achieve control we need to understand how our society operates. The groups (political, occupational, religious, educational and so on) which constitute it are expressions in practice of the major ideologies. As we come to understand these and the relations between them we come to understand our society and to know, at least within broad limits, what changes can be undertaken with a reasonable expectation of success. Ideological evolution continues, but with increasing understanding we can expect to bring it under control.

Meet Systematic Ideology

*I*deological *Commentary* announces itself as a journal of systematic ideology (s.i.), but it does not claim final knowledge of this theory; the formulation that looked like the ultimate last month needs alteration now, and the account given here undergoes continuing revision.

S.i. starts from observation of the limited success achieved by the reformers and revolutionaries (who themselves stress the failures of the traditionalists). After almost two centuries of struggle we still live under the familiar hierarchy and restraints; the conditions of life of the majority have not led them to support reform or revolution and do not seem likely to do so.

All political movements derive most of their support from those on the lower economic levels; only there do the necessary numbers appear. The significant difference between movements lies not in class position of the members but in their ideas, beliefs, values, assumptions. These tend to come in sets, and the sets of broad, general ideas etc. that appear in social life as the main political movements s.i. terms the major ideologies. The notes below list some of the features of these and indicate in outline some of the relations between them.

The Ideological Pyramid

The major ideologies, outlined on p. 178, have developed through history. Each of them provides the conditions which permit the next one to emerge, and each of them has fewer people attached to it than the one before. The diagram below indicates the outcome, the ideological structure of contemporary society, but the model needs to be used with caution; it presents no more than a bare outline, showing none of the complex internal relationships. Also, a pyramid is notably static, the ideological system dynamic. Different parts of it change at different rates, and for most social purposes its overall form can be taken as stable, but no part of it is permanently fixed and neither is the whole.

This pyramid forms the tip of the greater one representing universal evolution; there, also, the outcome is the total system, not any one level.

These ideologies, with the groups attached to them, form a hierarchy, but one of development, not of value, validity or influence; the anarchists, although at the top of the pyramid, neither exercise social domination nor seek to do so. Power is possessed and exercised mainly by the big numbers toward the foot. The bulk shown for each level indicates the relative influence exercised by that ideology.

The ideology of ideologies seems not to appear, but in fact it does; with each step upwards the concern with ideology strengthens, and in moving beyond repudiation it becomes total; the ideology of ideologies identifies not with any one level but with the whole system.

The pyramid on p. 177 is NOT TO SCALE; it seriously exaggerates the size and influence of the upper levels and understates the lower ones. From the base to the top of the pyramid there is increasing complexity in societies and people. Of the people reaching each stage many remain there; numbers, and consequently the influence exercised by the successive ideologies, diminish along the series. As each ideology develops the previous one, although continuing to influence behaviour, comes to be repressed and disvalued.

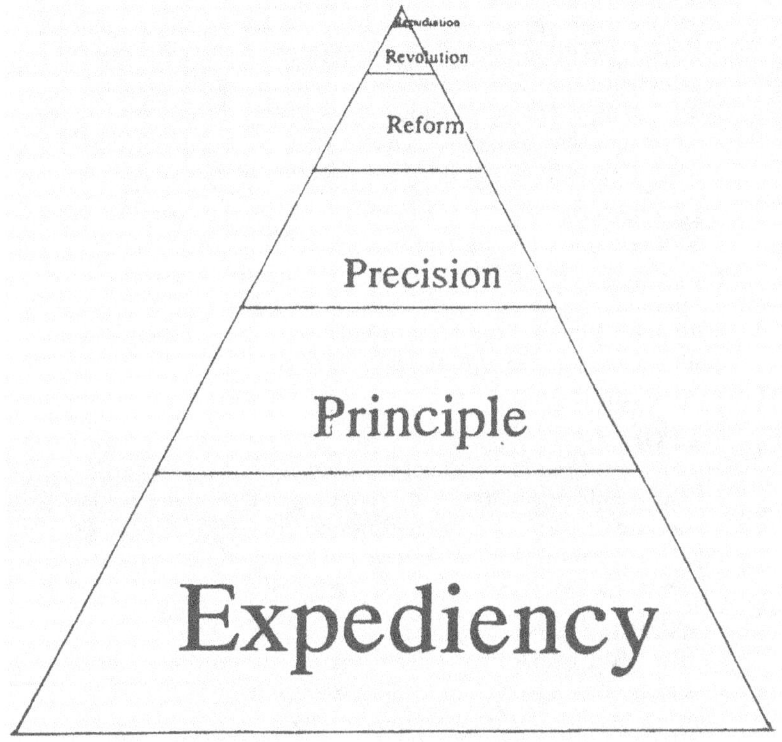
Repudiation
Revolution
Reform
Precision
Principle
Expediency

EDIOSTATIC

EXPEDIENCY

The only universal ideology; provides a criterion for selection among morally indifferent actions. Thinking unsystematised, the spiritual world polymorphous and not firmly distinguished from the material. Nonpolitical. Only foraging communities operate entirely in this way.

DOMINATION

Establishment, principle, the state, conventionality, commitment, devotion, discipline, authoritarian relation, social production. Thinking achieves firm (though not sharp) dualistic classification: good/bad, subject/ruler, sacred/secular. Compliance with the rules gives predictable behaviour, enabling large societies to function. Conservative politics.

PRECISION

'Hard' science, logic and accountancy. Ethics predominate over conformity and compliance, in religion as elsewhere. Humanism, agnosticism and freethinking begin to appear, with multiplicity, the 'billiard-ball' universe. Liberal in politics, greenism as a practical necessity.

EDIODYNAMIC

REFORM

Profound but gradual change; evolutionary science and gradualist socialism. Increasingly independent thinking leads sometimes to atheism, sometimes to mysticism, inspirational or esoteric religion: Internal interrelatedness. Holism appears, and greenism as an expression of it.

REVOLUTION

Sets its own values aggressively against conventional ones. Assumes classes to be in a conflict resolvable only by revolution, violent if need be; these social relations override other influences. Religion and greenism condemned as bourgeois misdirection of the workers.

REPUDIATION

Condemns all that has gone before, demanding immediate elimination of government, classes, religion and private ownership of the means of production, resulting in free access to goods in place of the exchange of commodities. Anarchist and anarcho-socialist.

IDEOLOGY OF IDEOLOGY

Recognises and accepts all of the above; has for its task resolution of the problems arising from their interaction.

An Outline Sketch of Systematic Ideology

An Outline Sketch of Systematic Ideology is a pamphlet published by George Walford in 1977. While *Beyond Politics* is intended to take the place of the *Outline*, it is included here to show how the theory has changed over time. The "Papers on Systematic Ideology" (p. 211) as well as many others can be found at gwiep.net.

- Trevor Blake

The Walsby Society

The Walsby Society is concerned with the theories of the late Harold Walsby. This pamphlet sketches Walsby's work in ideology; he also worked in other areas, notably in philosophy, mathematical logic, and the development of a dialectical algebra. His object, in all these studies, was to understand thought, thought itself and its effect upon the behaviour of people and of society.

The Walsby Society endeavours to carry on this work. It is a task which makes unusual demands upon those who would take part in it, for those who study thought must accept no restraints upon their own thinking. They must not regard any theory as proven, for this would be to exclude that theory from study. Those who would continue Walsby's work can accept even his own results only provisionally and tentatively. The greatest contribution anybody could make would be to prove all his results wrong; that would be a giant step forward along the path he strove to open up. The Walsby Society is concerned with Harold Walsby's work but is not committed to acceptance of it. All that is required of those who would work with the Society is that their activities should be relevant; opposition is as welcome as support.

This pamphlet is presented to the Walsby Society, but the Society has neither accepted nor rejected it. The Society, and the people connected with it, have complete freedom in regard to the propositions brought forward here, accepting or rejecting them as their own thinking shall indicate. The writer alone is responsible for every statement made.

So if this pamphlet should provoke you into opposing the theories it puts forward-well, that is one of the things it is meant to do. The Walsby Society will be glad to hear from you. Contact can probably be made through the source from which this pamphlet reached you. If not, then by writing to: The Bookshop, [address].

Introduction

The purpose of this essay is to present an outline sketch of the theory of ideology originated and developed by Harold Walsby. To present, not to establish. For support of what is set out here, for weight of evidence and answers to objections, the reader will need to look elsewhere, to its correspondence with his own experience, to Walsby's book, *The Domain of Ideologies*[1], or to the various works, papers and essays which undertake to establish different parts of the theory with argument and evidence[2]? My intention here is only to present a general framework. I hope to make it easier for the reader, particularly the newcomer to the subject, to appreciate the significance of the more specialised studies, to see where and how each of them fits in.

I should have liked to be able to claim that this essay, although limited in its aims, was accurate as far as it went. But this claim cannot be made. In reducing the complexity of ideological theory to this outline I have been unable to avoid distorting the outline itself. The reader will inevitably find, if he pursues his investigations, that as he encounters the material which has been excluded from this study it alters his view of what has been included. The most I can recommend is that the reader should treat this outline as a crutch, useful so long as he requires assistance but to be rejected when he has developed his own strength.

The theory of ideology to be presented is, with minor exceptions (and these, so far as it is possible to distinguish them, will be indicated), the work of Harold Walsby, who died in 1973. Walsby's starting-point was political. As a young man he was a revolutionary Socialist and, like others,

---

[1]Published by William MacLellan, Glasgow, in collaboration with The Social Science Association, 1947.

[2]These are listed on p. 211, "Papers on Systematic Ideology."

became frustrated by the ineffectiveness of the revolutionary Socialist movement, by its failure to attract the support of the masses whose interests it claimed to represent. Unlike most frustrated Socialists Walsby did not sink into apathy. Finding the theory of the Left inadequate, both as an explanation of political behaviour and as a guide to action, he turned to a re-examination of political ideas, beliefs and theories. He did not approach them in the manner in which one political thinker usually examines the work of another, in the hope of finding weak points. Neither did he examine them as a philosopher examines theories, with the purpose of distinguishing the true from the false. He approached them in the objective fashion of one wishing to understand how these things come to be. He examined the ideas, beliefs and theories themselves, the relationships between them, and their influence upon human behaviour. The result was his theory of ideology. This was in the late 1930's and the early 1940's, when "ideology" was a less familiar term than it is today.

Harold Walsby's book, *The Domain of Ideologies*, was published in 1947. Before that the two main landmarks in the field were *The German Ideology*, by Karl Marx and Friedrich Engels (written in 1845-1846 but not then published), and *Ideology and Utopia*, by Karl Mannheim (first published, in German, in 1929). During the last two decades there has been a growing stream of books and papers on ideology which do not derive from Walsby's work or, directly, from that of Marx and Engels, but rather from Mannheim. He was the first to set eyes on one large section of the mountain range of problems presented by ideology, but he did not succeed in crossing it, and I have not found that the workers following in his path have got much farther. I have not read all their works, but I have sampled them extensively; they refer widely to each other and I have found no indication, in those I have read, that the others are significantly different. Many of these works are largely concerned with the question whether all, or only some, political theories, movements or organisations are influenced by ideology. Nearly all of them take it for granted that the influence of ideology is restricted to the political, or at most the societal field. None of them shows, as Walsby does, that ideology influences the whole of our intentional or purposive behaviour in every field of activity. For those who may wish to enquire further the best starting point is the most recent of these books: *Ideology and Politics*, by Professor Martin Seliger, 1976. It is with the intention of distinguishing it from these other approaches to the subject, none of which display, or seem to be capable of developing, the degree of comprehensiveness and integration found in Walsby's work, that the term "systematic ideology" has recently been adopted for the Walsbeian theory.

Ideology and the Left

Walsby came to develop a theory of ideology which relates to all our purposive or intentional behaviour, but his starting-point was political. The immediate cause of his rejection of Left-wing political theory was the crucial perception that the Left is not a specifically working-class movement nor the Right a specifically capitalist or bourgeois one. It is of course true that the numerical support enjoyed by the Left comes mainly from the working class, but so does that enjoyed by the Right. In this respect the two movements are alike. In countries which have universal adult suffrage, freedom of speech, of publication and political organisation, the Right consistently receives from the electorate, which is overwhelmingly of the working class, a number of votes which is at least comparable with, and is sometimes greater than, the number of votes received by the Left. The political division between Left and Right does not correspond with the economic division between workers and capitalists (or bourgeoisie) and, even after generations of Left-wing propaganda, is not coming to do so. The political struggles which occur in industrial or post-industrial states cannot be understood so long as they are assumed to be, or to reflect, or to express, struggles between economic classes. When political conflict becomes violent the battle is rarely, if ever, between capitalists and workers. It is Workers of the Left and workers of the Right who shoot one another.

The responsible spokesmen and thinkers of the Left are rarely so simpleminded as to claim that political allegiance is

directly determined by class position; rather do they emphasise their rejection of "economic determinism." But they do
assume some significant connection between the Left and the
working class, although most of them are reluctant to specify
exactly what it is (and those who do attempt to do so contradict each other). The Left is regarded as the working-class
movement, having for opponent the Right, which is the movement of the capitalists, or the bourgeoisie, or the bosses. The
Left account for political behaviour, however indirectly and
with whatever refinements, by reference to the relationships
between economic classes.

Walsby's work indicates that this view is not valid, that
political conflicts cannot be understood in terms of the relationships between economic classes, that there is no significant
correlation, direct or indirect, between the political structure
of our society and its economic class structure. His explanation of the political structure which tends to appear, always
displaying the same broad features, in every industrial or
post-industrial country where universal adult suffrage and
political freedom obtain, is that it is the expression, in the
political field, of an ideological structure. The adherents of
each political position extend over the whole range of economic positions. There are Right-wing workers and there are
Left-wing capitalists. The adherents of each political position
are not united by a common class position or a common
economic interest. They are united by sharing a common
ideology. We shall see that this means a good deal more
than the self-evident proposition that the adherents of each
political position have certain political ideas in common.

The Field of Ideology
The term "ideology," like the term "psychology," is used with
three distinct meanings. It refers to that which is studied, to
the activity of studying it, and to the theory resulting from
that study. (Also, by analogy with "psychologist," we shall
refer to the student of ideology as an ideologist).

Ideology (that which is studied) cannot be directly observed; its presence is inferred from observation of behaviour.
It is, of course, by this means that we arrive at all our knowl-

184

edge of the various structures internal to the living human being. We observe that what appears to be soft flesh maintains its form under stress, and from this we infer the presence of a rigid skeleton. We see that the emotional responses of each person are not random, and are not entirely determined by the stimuli applied, and from this we infer the presence of an emotional structure. We observe that the volitional behaviour, the considered statements and the purposeful actions, of each person are relatively predictable and consistent, and from this we infer the presence of a structure of ideas (a phrase which we will accept, for the moment, as referring to an ideology). In each instance, in order to render the observed behaviour comprehensible, we are obliged to infer the presence of an internal structure which significantly influences an area or class of behaviour. This willingness to recognise that action is significantly affected by internal factors, their presence implied by observable behaviour, is one of the things that distinguishes Walsby's approach from that of the behaviourists.

The behaviour which is influenced by ideology is volitional or intentional behaviour, the actions we perform upon consideration or with purpose. It is not necessary, for any action to be included in this field, that the consideration involved should be deep or prolonged, or the purpose a long-term one. If I move my lower leg as a reflex action after being struck below the knee that is not an item of volitional behaviour and is not influenced by my ideology. But if I perform exactly the same movement with the purpose of kicking a ball that is volitional behaviour and is influenced by my ideology. It is not necessary that the thought connected with the action should be valid. Men regulated their actions, over thousands of years, in accordance with theories which have since been proven false. Their actions rank, none the less, as intentional and purposive, their behaviour comes within the field of ideology.

See also *Domain of Ideologies* Part II Chapter 1.

Assumption and Identification
The twin foundation stones of ideological theory are the associated concepts of assumption and identification.

Assumption: Ideology is one of the studies concerned with thought, and it is general practice, among those who study thinking, to distinguish between the true and the false. It is, indeed, often taken for granted that the establishment of this distinction is the object and end of all such studies. The first hurdle which the ideologist has to surmount is that this distinction, if taken as an absolute one, is itself false. It is only relatively true. Nothing is absolutely true and nothing is absolutely false. All our knowledge, taking that term in its widest sense, to include not only facts but also theories, principles, opinions and so on, is relatively true, and all of it is relatively false. We do not know anything with unqualified, absolute certainty; there is no alleged fact which cannot be challenged, there is no proof which cannot be questioned. However strong the evidence there is always something pointing in the contrary direction, even if it be only the possibility of conceiving that things might be otherwise. The distinction between false and true, and also the distinction between what we know and what we "merely" assume, is a distinction only of degree. All our knowledge consists of assumptions, some of them more true than others, some of them better supported than others, but none absolutely true and none established with final and absolute certainty.

By accepting this the ideologist is relieved of the intolerable burden of deciding, for every proposition he encounters, whether it is true or false.

He knows in advance that it is an assumption, relatively true and relatively false, with some evidence in its favour and some against it. Knowing this, he can move on to examine its relationships with other assumptions and – his particular concern – its effects upon behaviour. When one is concerned to understand how assumptions influence behaviour then their truth or falsity is commonly irrelevant; men can be moved quite as powerfully by false assumptions as by true ones. Sometimes the degree of truth or falsity possessed by an assumption may be relevant, and then the ideologist is free to determine it, by the well-tried method of assembling and balancing the evidence on each side. But he is not bound to carry out this procedure – it is often a lengthy and difficult one – in every case before he can perform any other operations upon the assumption in question.

Ideology is concerned with our volitional behaviour, the actions we perform with purpose, and every action of this type implies the presence of assumptions. By acting in a certain way we show that we assume the situation in which we find ourselves to possess certain features.

As I sit here typing my behaviour implies that I assume the chair is strong enough to support me, the floor strong enough to support the chair, the joists the floor, and so on; a series of assumptions leading, eventually, to assumptions concerning the nature of matter and of the universe. All these assumptions are implied by my behaviour in sitting in the chair; if I did not make them I would not behave as I do, I would not sit in a chair if I did not assume it to be adequately supported.

At any time some assumptions are present to awareness and others are not, and rarely, if ever, can an action be fully explained by reference to assumptions of which the actor is aware. Assumptions not present to awareness are nearly always involved. Every time I speak to a person my behaviour implies the assumptions on my part that his hearing is good (which itself implies long chains of assumptions concerning his anatomy and physiology), that he understands the language I use (another long chain of assumptions concerning his education), that his attention is not concentrated elsewhere, that there is air between us to carry the vibrations produced by my vocal cords, that there is no louder noise to drown my voice, and so on – and on and on. This one common act implies assumptions almost without end[1]. All these assumptions are implied by my behaviour, but most of them are not present to my awareness. They cannot be; my capacity for awareness is limited, it cannot contain them all; it cannot even contain many of them without excluding that which I wish to speak about. Many, probably by far the greater part of the assumptions which are implied by, and which influence, our behaviour are necessarily not present to our awareness.

---

[1] *The Domain of Ideologies* pp. 155-6.

Identification: We do not treat our assumptions as matters purely of logic, reason and evidence. We do not necessarily abandon an assumption because we have been compelled to admit that it runs against the balance of evidence, or is in contradiction either with itself or some other of our assumptions. We are not indifferent about our assumptions, we are attached to them.

A person is a whole comprising (among other features) a body and an ideology. Bodily experience affects the ideology – my experiences when I try to walk through a brick wall affect my assumptions concerning the nature of matter. Also, ideological structure affects physical behaviour – because my political assumptions have been changed I read different books and attend different meetings.

This interaction between body and ideology shows that, although distinct, they form parts of a whole, a whole we term a person, or a self. When our bodies are injured we say: "I was hurt," and similarly when our assumptions are attacked, we say: "He said I was wrong." Our behaviour implies that we regard our assumptions as parts of our selves, that we identify them with our selves, and our selves with them.

Identifications may be strong or weak. I have an assumption concerning the time of day, but my identification with it is weak; only a small amount of evidence – a glance at the clock – is required for me to abandon it and adopt another in its place. There are other assumptions to which I am strongly attached. It would take a great deal of evidence to induce me to abandon the assumption that I have, up till now at least, had two hands. In one case the attachment is weak, in the other it is strong, but both are, in ideological terminology, identifications.

"Assumption" and "identification" are used in systematic ideology as technical terms, and they are as neutral as any term in physical science. They state the presence of that to which they refer, and nothing more. With one exception, anything we may wish to convey about the strength, validity or other features of the assumption or identification in question must be explicitly added. The exception is that unless otherwise stated "identification" refers to a positive identification; if the one being referred to is negative it is necessary to say so. Some assumptions we favour, or support, or accept; others we disfavour, or oppose, or repudiate. In each case our behaviour is affected by the assumption; in each case we are attached to it, identified with it. But in one case the identification is positive, in the other it is negative.

There is one aspect of the behaviour connected with identification which can be misleading if one is not prepared for it. Completely positive identification with an assumption does not appear as enthusiastic support for it, and completely negative identification with an assumption does not appear as determined opposition to it. Support implies a distinction between supporter and supported, and hence something short of complete positive identification. Equally, opposition implies a connection between opposer and opposed, and hence something short of complete negative identification. Completely positive identification appears as unquestioning taking-for-granted, and completely negative identification appears as complete detachment from the assumption in question.

Most identifications are not completely positive or completely negative but only relatively one or the other. When the ideologist speaks of a positive or negative identification he means one which is relatively so; if the identification is completely negative or completely positive it is necessary to specify this.

When we support an assumption we imply that we are positively identified with it, and when we oppose one we imply that we are negatively identified with it. All identifications are either positive or negative, but many are not strongly one or the other, and for these the terms "support" and "opposition" may be too definite. There are a number of terms which can be used to describe the behaviour implying one or another degree of positivity or negativity, two of the most useful being "acceptance" and "concern." Acceptance of something implies positive identification with it, and a concern with something implies negative identification with it.

Thus the scientist is concerned with phenomena which are not understood, or not fully so, and this is a negative identification. His concern diminishes as understanding increases, and with the phenomena which are (or are believed to be) fully understood, so that he can accept them, his identification is positive.

When we say that concern indicates negative identification we are implying that a supporter of a movement, one whose identification with it is positive, is not concerned with it. This may contradict the usual view of the situation, but when we look more closely we see it is justified. The supporter does not wish to change the movement – if he did, he would not be an unqualified supporter. He accepts the movement as it is, is not concerned about it. What he wishes to change is the resistance the movement meets. He is opposed to this resistance, negatively identified with it, and it is with this resistance that he is concerned.

Definition of an Ideology

An ideology is usually thought of rather vaguely, as a person's system of ideas, or set of beliefs or values, or his general outlook, or mental attitude. We are now able to define it more sharply, as the set of assumptions with which he is identified.

Or, in Walsby's more extended definition:

> (An ideology is) the complete system of cognitive assumptions and affective identifications which manifest themselves in, or underlie, the thought, speech, aims, interests, ideals, ethical standards, actions – in short, the behaviour – of an individual human being![1]

Ideological Groups

Each of us has his own unique ideology, his system of identifications and assumptions, which is not the same as that of anybody else. Also, some of the particular assumptions within each unique set are peculiar to the person concerned. Each of us has, for example, assumptions concerning his own body which he shares with nobody else. But each unique, personal set contains, in addition to particular assumptions, also more general assumptions, and these are held in common with

---

[1] *The Domain of Ideologies*, p. 145.

other people. People identified with the same assumptions are thereby constituted an ideological group.

Some ideological groups are small, some are large. Their size depends primarily upon the generality of the assumptions which form the basis for the group, and the larger groups tend to be the more enduring. Thus the assumption "England" is more general than the assumption of any one address in England, and the group of people identified with England is both larger and more enduring than the group identified with any one English address.

It is common for assumptions to be included one within the other, as in this example, and sometimes this relationship extends through a series, producing a "Chinese-box" pattern of assumptions and also of the groups identified with them.

I assume I have pennies, you assume you have pound notes, and he assumes he has five-pound notes; no two of us have the same particular assumption. But we are all identified with the same general assumption: we all assume we have some English money. This common identification constitutes us an ideological group, and also distinguishes that group from another, composed of those identified with the assumption that they have some French money. These two groups, (together with other "national-money" groups) form a larger group whose members are identified with the more general assumption that they have some European money. As the assumptions become more general, so the groups become larger and fewer.

As one moves from more particular assumptions toward more general ones (and, accordingly, from smaller toward larger ideological groups), there comes a stage at which the assumptions and identifications under consideration are sufficiently general that each set, forming the basis of an ideological group, embraces, or is capable of being related to, the whole of existence, to the totality of both the social and the non-social worlds. At this level of generality the number of sets of assumptions, and consequently the number of ideological groups into which the population is divided, is small, and it is mainly these groups which are significant for the understanding of political behaviour. We shall refer to these universal systems of assumptions and identifications as "the major ideologies."

The Major Ideologies

Each of the major ideologies is capable of being expressed in relation to any field of existence, in relation to man, the natural world, the physical universe, the realm of ideas, and so on. In the field of abstract thought they appear as the different major philosophies (or classes of philosophies), and they can also be recognised as underlying the various religions, sciences, theories of art, etcetera. In relation to society they have been more fully developed than in some other fields, and here they appear as the familiar major political positions.

The main components of each of these systems of highly general assumptions have been distinguished, and it is accordingly possible to study, so to speak, the major ideologies "themselves," independently of their expressions in relation to particular fields of activity. They are seven in number and are entitled, respectively: protostatic, epistatic, parastatic, protodynamic, epidynamic, paradynamic, metadynamic[1]. As these names indicate, one of the main features by which each of them is distinguished is its assumption concerning the predominance of one or another form of the static or the dynamic principle in the world, and we shall discuss them firstly from this angle, taking the opportunity at the same time to indicate the political viewpoint especially associated with each ideology.

Protostatic: Those identified with this ideology imply by their behaviour their identification with the assumption that reality is static (or would be so if it were not interfered with). The only changes acceptable are those seen as tending to produce a static condition. The declaration by the Nazis of their intention to establish a state which should endure unchanged for a thousand years was calculated to obtain support from the protostatics[2].

Epistatic: Those identified with this ideology imply by their behaviour their identification with the assumption that although reality is predominantly static (or would be so if

---

[1]These terms were not used by Walsby: they are a recent introduction.

[2]The protostatic ideology is very much more important than appears from this brief notice; *The Domain of Ideologies* Part I is largely devoted to it.

it were not interfered with) yet the static situation is often most effectively preserved by compromise with the dynamic principle. This ideology appears in the political field as Conservatism[1], with its willingness to accept changes which are in accordance with tradition or the wish of the people generally, or which will tend to avert greater changes. The attitude of Conservatism toward change can perhaps be described as reluctant flexibility.

Parastatic: Those identified with this ideology imply by their behaviour their identification with the assumption that change is a necessary part of existence but within a static framework. Changes are freely accepted, even promoted, provided they are improvements or adjustments, not affecting the basis of the structure concerned or the essence of the situation. This ideology appears in politics as Liberalism, which is concerned with progress, with perfecting the present social system, but is not concerned to transform this system into a different one.

With the three ideologies above, and the groups identified with them, we have a situation we have met before. Each of them has its own particular assumption concerning the form or degree of staticism which predominates in the world, but all of them are identified with the general assumption that it is the static and not the dynamic principle which predominates. Accordingly these three ideological groups together form a larger group; this group, and the ideology with which it is identified, Walsby terms eidostatic.

The next three major ideological groups are each identified with their own assumptions concerning the form or degree of the dynamic principle which predominates in the world; each of them is identified with the general assumption that it is the dynamic and not the static principle which is predominant, and accordingly these three ideological groups together also form one larger one; this group, and the ideology with which

---

[1]Throughout this paper names of political parties or movements are to be read as: "The party (or movement) which is known in Britain as... " The ideological equivalents are to be found in all industrial or post-industrial states where they are not suppressed, but they commonly bear different names and often exhibit other differences also. It is partly in order to avoid losing our main theme in these complications that this paper is written largely in terms of Left and Right.

it is identified, Walsby terms eidodynamic[1].

Protodynamic: Those identified with this ideology imply by their behaviour their assumption that change is (or ought to be) universal and that it is (or ought to be) gradual, evolutionary rather than revolutionary. This ideology appears in politics as Labour-Socialism.

Epidynamic: Those identified with this ideology imply by their behaviour their identification with the assumption that change is (or ought to be) universal and fundamental, the appearance that anything may give of being static being a superficial illusion. Change, furthermore, is (or should be) not merely gradual and continuous but includes also discontinuities, revolutions, and it is changes of this type which are most highly valued. This ideology appears in politics as Communism.

Paradynamic: Those identified with this ideology imply by their behaviour their identification with the assumption that change is (or ought to be) universal and abolitionary. The state should not be maintained, adjusted, reformed or revolutionised, but abolished. This ideology appears in politics as Anarchism.

Each of the six groups mentioned above tends to assume that its own ideology is wholly and exclusively true. Like other assumptions this is more often implied than directly expressed. In politics the members of each group endeavour to establish a form of society which shall embody only their own assumptions. In other areas the members of each group assume or endeavour to demonstrate the exclusive validity of views or theories expressing their own assumptions, and to show that those expressing other assumptions are unscientific, or false, or wicked, according to the categories used in the particular field of activity.

Evidently, it is not possible that every one of these major ideologies should be wholly and exclusively true. If one is true then the others are false, or if all are relatively true then all are relatively false. But each ideology, and each assumption of each ideology, influences the behaviour of the group identified

---

[1] *The Domain of Ideologies* Part II Chapter 7.

with it, confirming something mentioned earlier: the power of an assumption to influence behaviour does not depend upon its truth.

There is still one more major ideology to be brought forward:

Metadynamic: Those identified with this ideology imply by their behaviour that they are not exclusively identified with any one of the various forms of either the static or the dynamic principle but with all of them.

A short diversion is necessary, to avoid appearing wilfully mysterious. Although we do not go into the question in this essay, each of the major ideologies is particularly fitted, by correspondence between its basic assumptions and the basic structure of a certain field of existence, to perform a certain part of the total range of activities needed for the effective functioning of the social organisation[1]. The sphere of existence with which the metadynamic group is, by the nature of its basic assumptions, particularly associated, is the ideological field itself. This group, being concerned with the study of ideologies, is not identified with this or that assumption concerning a particular form of the static or the dynamic principle but with all the assumptions concerning either of them exhibited by the other major ideologies. In the field of politics this ideology does not appear as a separate movement or organisation but as a concern with the relationships between the other major ideologies, their political expressions, and the groups identified with them. The presence of the metadynamic ideology also answers the question whether there can be further ideologies extending the range beyond those given here; the answer is, briefly, that at this point the series returns upon itself. There is little point in going into further details here since the whole of this essay is an exposition of the metadynamic ideology.

---

[1]This was clearly implied in Walsby's work but, apart from some brief references, was not made explicit. It has recently begun to be developed, mainly, so far, in *The Enduring Eidostatics.* I emphasise here that the functional division between ideologies does not correspond to the division between economic classes.

Ideological Development

The order in which the major ideologies have been presented, running from protostatic to metadynamic, is not an arbitrary one. This is the order in which they succeed each other in the development of the individual. We all begin life as protostatics, some remain in this phase and others become epistatics. Some remain in this phase and others become parastatics, and so on through the series. With each step some of the limitations of the previous phase are overcome and some new limitations are incurred, and each step involves the attempt to repudiate the assumptions of the previous phase[1]. Walsby traces the origins of this process in the early experiences of the growing child[2] but we shall confine our attention to its appearance in political and societal behaviour.

When we first emerge from family life into direct contact with the general social system we have little or no historical perspective. We are aware that things are happening around us, people moving and events occurring, but we have no reason to assume that the general structure of society is changing. Neither, of course, do we consciously assume it to be static; the question does not directly arise. But our behaviour in this phase implies that we make the static assumption. When young we do not readily think of our parents as having once been children, and still less are we able to accept that the conditions of childhood in their youth may have been different from those we have known. We all begin societal life with the static assumption, we first encounter the world as protostatics.

Many of us retain this primary, more or less unqualified, identification with the static principle throughout our lives, continuing to behave as though the general structure of society never changed. Others find that as their experience grows they are obliged to accept that significant changes in this structure do occur; changes, for example, in laws and economic relationships. To this recognition there are two possible responses; the list confirms the person in his protostatic identification, the second takes him into the next phase of

---

[1]This attempt is never wholly successful; see *Economic Individualism and Collectivism* below.

[2]*Domain of Ideologies* Part II Chapter 7.

development.

The first of the two possible responses to the recognition of change is to maintain identification with the static principle but now to engage in active defence of it. Those who exhibit this response no longer merely take the static principle for granted. Rather do they assert that the static principle is the right one, that the dynamic principle is evil and to be resisted. This response, this active assertion of the protostatic ideology, leads toward efforts to eliminate the assumed causes of change – Jews, immigrants and agitators for example. Here we have the root of the connection between the protostatic ideology and autocratic or totalitarian movements; these all strive for elimination of influences assumed to be making for change. (I emphasise that not all protostatics behave in this way. It is also possible for the protostatic not to recognise the existence of significant change, to maintain his passive identification with the static assumption, and observation shows this to be a common stance. The protostatic ideology is not to be equated with Nazism or with Fascism).

The protostatic may recognise the existence of significant societal change or he may not. If he does recognise it he may change from a passive mode to an active one; he may start trying to prevent change and to eliminate the assumed causes of it. In either case he maintains his identification with the protostatic ideology. But there is another response open to him. He may recognise the existence of societal change and accept it, come to regard it as something real and necessary. In this case he ceases to be a protostatic and moves to the next phase of ideological development.

The person surrendering his identification with the protostatic assumptions does not, however, leap directly to full acceptance of the dynamic principle. He has taken only the first step on a long journey. The change in his ideology is a minimal one, extending only to the recognition that it is well to be somewhat flexible in the matter, that to maintain the static principle rigidly is often to ensure its defeat, and that it can best be defended by admitting, under careful control, some small element of dynamism. The protostatic becomes an epistatic, he comes to identify with the major ideology which appears in the political field as Conservatism, accepting such changes as are in accordance with tradition, or will serve to avoid greater changes, and displaying towards the static-dynamic issue, as in other connections, a willingness to compromise.

The epistatic phase is not the end of the process. Some do remain in this phase but others move on to the parastatic ideology. The process can be followed (although with some complications) through the whole ideological series to the metadynamic phase, but enough has been said to enable us to bring out the point with which we are immediately concerned. This is that the presence, in the ideology of a person, of a modified form of the static assumption, implies that he was previously identified with an unmodified form of it. The nature of the epistatic ideology implies that those identified with it were previously identified with the protostatic. When the major ideologies are arranged in the order: protostatic, epistatic, parastatic, protodynamic, epidynamic, paradynamic, metadynamic, then the presence of a person at any point in the series shows him to have passed through the preceding phases.

One point which arises here is that we see ideology to be more than a complicated way of putting things that could equally well be expressed in political terms. It is, obviously, not the case that every Anarchist has been a Communist, every Communist a Labour Socialist, and so on. What ideological theory tells us is that every person identified with any ideology in the series from protostatic to metadynamic has been previously identified with the preceding ones in the series. He may or may not have expressed any of these identifications in the political field.

Intellect

As one moves along the range from protostatic toward metadynamic so the original identification with the static principle comes to be replaced by identification with dynamism.

There are other ideological features which follow a similar course of development as one moves along the ideological range, and in the next section we shall briefly discuss some of these, not following out their full development from one major ideology to the next but indicating the general course followed by each feature through the ideological series. These features are the identification with intellect, the group and cosmic situations, and individualism and collectivism, political and economic. I begin with intellect.

The identification with intellect and intellectuality is negative at the protostatic end of the range and becomes positive as one approaches the metadynamic. Nazism repudiates intellect and intellectuality, Anarchism accepts them[1]. It is necessary to distinguish between "intellect" and "intelligence[2]." The relationship between the two is complex and difficult, and they are commonly confused. All I can do here is to stress that ideological theory does not suggest that those toward the protostatic end of the range are any less intelligent, less sharp or quick of mind (or less capable of acquiring knowledge) than those toward the metadynamic end. What it asserts is that the former tend to accept non-rational factors as guides to action while the latter are concerned that their behaviour should be logically consistent and capable of being justified by reason.

Nazism (protostatic) claims to be guided by non-intellectual factors such as blood, race, the Will of the Leader. Toward the other extreme Anarchists (paradynamic) take it for granted that their behaviour should be governed by intellectual considerations; they devote much time and effort to study, argument and discussion, to ensuring that their behaviour shall be intellectually justifiable. The intervening ideologies display greater or lesser concern with intellect according to their situation in the range, the epistatic or Conservative, for example, being more intellectual than the protostatic or Fascist but less so than the epidynamic or Communist, who in turn is less so than the paradynamic or Anarchist.

The Group Situation

The environment in which we live can be divided in many ways. For the ideologist one significant division is between

---

[1] *Domain of Ideologies* Part I Chapters 3, 4.
[2] *Domain of Ideologies* pages 28-31.

the social group and the rest of the environment. The two main ideological classes, eidostatic and eidodynamic, each display a characteristic pair of identifications, one with the social group (Walsby terms this the group situation), and the converse identification with the environment external to the social group (Walsby terms this the cosmic situation)[1].

The eidodynamics (Socialists, Communists, Anarchists) regard the existing social structure as the main source of the ills from which we suffer. They do not ascribe war, poverty, insecurity and the rest to the will of God, or the natural aggressiveness of man, or to natural law, or to any other extra-social factor, but to "the contradictions of capitalism" or some other feature of our social organisation. They maintain that in order to improve human conditions we must reform, revolutionise or abolish existing society. They experience existing society as a hostile presence. They are opposed to it. They exhibit negative identification with it. As, in the Anarchist phase, this identification approaches complete negativity it tends to turn from concern into repudiation; Anarchists are not interested in the possibilities of reforming, or even of revolutionising, existing society. They would abolish it.

The eidostatics appearing in the political field as the Right exhibit the converse attitude toward the existing social structure. They are positively identified with it. We mentioned earlier that positive identification, when complete, does not appear as enthusiastic support. Active support implies recognition of a distinction between supporter and supported, and hence something short of a completely positive identification. Those most completely identified with their social group (in this connection usually the nation), are not the outspoken patriots but those who take their membership of the group, and their compliance with the implied conditions of membership, completely for granted, and it is those at the eidostatic end of the range, the protostatics, who tend to behave in this way.

Among the more moderate eidostatics, the Conservatives and Liberals, the identification is less exclusively positive;

---

[1] *Domain of Ideologies* pp. 212 *et seq.*

there is some tendency toward recognising the group as something distinct from the person and, consequently, for the decision to support it to become a conscious choice. But even in this phase the social structure is not seen as the decisive factor in the human condition. Rich and poor alike, the Right tend to regard poverty as a result of extra-social factors – natural law, luck, personal qualities or the will of God – and consequently as something which just has to be accepted. They do not see poverty as the Left do, as a result of specific social conditions which can be altered. As Dr. Johnson expressed it: "How small, of all that human hearts endure / The part that laws or kings can cause or cure." This assumption is clearly distinct from the one with which the Left are identified, that laws, if not kings, can cause or cure a great deal.

In connection with the existing social structure, as elsewhere, negative identification tends to produce active concern, moving toward repudiation, and eventually detachment, as the identification becomes completely negative, and positive identification tends to appear as acceptance, becoming unquestioning as the identification approaches complete positivity.

The Cosmic Situation

When we turn to consider the respective identifications of the two main ideological classes with the non-social world (what Walsby terms their cosmic situations), we find a reversal of the identifications which they respectively exhibit with existing society. The eidostatics, (positively identified with existing society), are negatively identified with the non-social world, and the eidodynamics, (negatively identified with existing society), are positively identified with the non-social world.

The Left regard existing society as the source of poverty, insecurity, war, and the other major ills from which we suffer. They regard the non-social world in much the same way as the Right regard the social, as something presenting no particular problems and exercising no very great effect, either for good or ill. They are, for example, greatly concerned with poverty. In combating it they concentrate their efforts upon ensuring a more equitable distribution of the commodities available (an intra-social matter) rather than upon producing a greater supply of commodities (an activity directed toward the non-social world, the source of raw materials). Their behaviour implies that they assume the non-social world to be so far under control that it presents no serious problems. As they sometimes phrase it: "the problem of production has been solved." The Left, the eidodynamics, display toward the non-social world that attitude of acceptance, of taking for granted, that we have come to recognise as indicative of positive identification.

The eidostatics, on the contrary, tend to see the non-social world as the source of the ills from which we suffer, and accordingly it is toward this world that their efforts are mainly directed. They tend to concern themselves with efforts to establish and exercise control of the non-social world, sometimes by prayer, sometimes by industry. They concern themselves with the production of goods, an activity directed toward the non-social world, rather than with questions concerning the fairness of their distribution within society. Toward the non-social world the Right display that active concern which we recognise as indicative of a negative identification.

Political Individualism and Collectivism

The ideologist does not dispute the general opinion that the ideas of the Right are different from those of the Left, but he does add something to it. Right and Left, eidostatics and eidodynamics, not only have different ideas, they also have different ways of thinking. As Walsby phrases it, they differ not only in the content but also in the form of their thought. The thinking of the Right tends toward agreement, toward acceptance of the prevailing opinion and toward compliance with authority. It tends toward fusion. The thinking of the Left tends in the opposite direction, toward disagreement, independence of thought, and resistance to authority. It tends toward fission.

These tendencies Walsby names, respectively, political (as distinct from economic) collectivism and political individualism. As is commonly the case with the features which distinguish the various ideologies, each of them is to be observed in the purest form toward the appropriate end of the range, political collectivism among protostatics and autocratic movements, political individualism among extreme eidodynamics.

The intermediate ideologies exhibit a greater or lesser tendency toward political collectivism or political individualism according to their position in the range. Nazism was explicitly and emphatically opposed to political individualism. The establishment of a totalitarian state required the elimination of independent thinking. The Nazis burnt books, imposed political control on the teaching given in the universities, killed, suppressed or expelled those holding political beliefs other than their own, and suppressed or banished those displaying mental independence even in what might appear to be neutral fields, such as art and literature.

In ideological terms they endeavoured to suppress all ideologies other than the protostatic. Nazism exhibited, in a virulent form, the absence of restraint, the identification with unmodified assumptions, characteristic of the protostatic phase. As one moves away from this end of the range through the more moderately eidostatic phases, epistatic and parastatic, the identification with political collectivism, and the opposition to political individualism, becomes less intense. Freedom of the press and of research come to be accepted, tolerance and the rule of law replace the demand that the individual should submit without reservation to the state. But even in these phases there is no doubt which way the balance of identification lies. Among Conservatives and among Liberals the assumption is that tradition, loyalty and submission to authority should take precedence over independent thinking as guides to action, and these are all forms of political collectivism.

This contrasts with the behaviour exhibited at the eidodynamic end of the range. As we move from Labour-Socialism, through Communism to Anarchism, so the tendency towards, and the influence of, collective thinking diminishes and independent thinking comes increasingly to be accepted as a valid guide to social action, until with Anarchism it becomes explicit that the individual is to be subjected to no authority or influence whatever, but is to decide his own course of action for himself.

One apparent anomaly needs mentioning. It is in the Communist movement, rather than among the eidostatics, that supporters are required to accept a prescribed "party line" under pain of disciplinary action, and this may seem to run against our connection of the eidodynamic ideologies with independent thinking. We need only comment that the eidostatic organisations do not need to impose such a requirement; their members rarely display a tendency toward independent thought strong enough to need restraining.

The term "individual" usually means an individual person, but this is not the only sense in which it may be used. We may equally well speak of individual families, individual parties, movements, firms, teams, crowds and so on. We may speak not only of biological but also of social individuals. Every distinct group is a social individual, and in political affairs (and also in economic affairs) it is these, rather than the biological individuals, which are the relevant units, the biological individual being a special case, a group consisting of one member. The proposition, therefore, that political individualism is exhibited by the eidodynamics, is not invalidated by the observation that Communists, or Anarchists, although perhaps displaying greater personal independence of thought than do Liberals, or Conservatives, yet accept the same general assumptions as other Communists or Anarchists, and to this extent may be said to think collectively. It is not only the Communists and Anarchists as separate persons who display political individuality, but also the Communist and Anarchist movements. Where the eidostatic movements tend to be supportive of the general society and, in time of stress, to submerge in it such individuality as they may at other times exhibit, the eidodynamic movements, Socialism, Communism and Anarchism set themselves up against the general society and the more extreme of them, at least, continue this opposition even in time of stress, as when the continued existence of the community is threatened by an enemy. They behave toward it (and also toward each other) as separate individuals.

See also *Domain of Ideologies* Part I Chapter 6 and 7.

Economic Individualism and Collectivism

In the economic field the situation of the ideologies, as regards collectivism and individualism, is the reverse of that in the political field. The eidostatics exhibit economic individualism and the eidodynamics exhibit economic collectivism.

It is commonly accepted that the transition, which is occurring in Britain and other western democracies (and which has already occurred in the Communist countries), from private ownership of the mills, mines, factories and other major components of the productive system, to their ownership by the state and control by bodies representing the state, is a change from capitalism to (or toward) socialism. This may or may not be so; it depends on the meaning given to "socialism." What is definite is that this transition is not a change from economic individualism to economic collectivism. In the economic field as in the political field, the individuals in question are groups; there they were parties or movements, here they are firms, corporations, boards, industries. The change from ownership and control by independent persons (so far as that system ever existed; most economic organisations of any size always have been owned and controlled by groups) to state ownership and control by groups appointed by the state, is a change from one form of economic individualism to another. The various boards, corporations and so on which operate "state capitalism" and similar systems are just as much separate individuals – mutually exclusive, often competitive and sometimes hostile individuals – as the individual capitalists or individual boards of directors ever were. They act as independent individuals toward each other, toward the community as a whole, and toward each member of the community.

Economic collectivism is (or rather, if it were ever to be established on any large scale it would be) something different from this. It is a system whereby the means of production as a whole are owned and controlled by society as a whole, each person having free access to the means of production (and hence to their products) by virtue of his membership of the owning and controlling community.

Personal Ideological Structure

Any reader who accepts – even if only provisionally – the theories brought forward in the preceding pages, and sets out to test them against his own observations, will quickly encounter gross discrepancies. The protostatics present no great problem; it will be found that their behaviour does, if not in all details then at least when taken as a whole, or over a period, exhibit predominantly the features these theories would lead us to expect. The first indication of trouble is the observation that the adherents of all other ideologies display, for much of the time and over large areas of activity, behaviour which is indistinguishable from that of the protostatics.

We all spend much time in eating, travelling, casual conversation, watching films or television, engaging in sports or attending entertainments (Friedrich Engels was a keen foxhunter), and these are all activities which imply identification with protostatic assumptions, with low intellectuality and political collectivism. Even in the act of verbally expressing our eidodynamic assumptions we have no choice but to demonstrate our protostatic identification with the general social group; we are obliged to use the common speech.

As one enquires further the discrepancies between theory and observation become more extensive. Each of the major ideological groups behaves in a way implying identification not only with its own ideology but also with all ideologies lying to the protostatic side of its own position. The discrepancy between ideological theory (as so far presented), and observable behaviour, becomes more severe as attention moves toward the eidodynamic end of the range until, with the paradynamics, we find that the behaviour predicted by theory is, for some of them, a rare occurrence in their lives. Quite often we would need to spend long periods, sometimes years, observing the behaviour, including the speech, of a paradynamic before encountering any item of behaviour implying identification with the assumptions we have listed as distinctive of this ideology.

The difficulty is resolved when we take into account a feature which ideological development shares with some other developmental systems. This is that the development is from less to more complex, one aspect of the increasing complexity being the retention, within each successive phase as it emerges, of the main features of the less complex phases in the system. Thus the broadest of all developmental systems moves from the physical through the organic to the human; in this system man is the most complex phase, and he is so partly because he is not merely, or purely, human but incorporates also the main features of the organic and physical phases. He is a man and an animal and a physical object. In the ideological series each phase beyond the protostatic is not merely, or purely, epistatic, or parastatic, and so on, but is epistatic and protostatic, parastatic and epistatic and protostatic, until, at the eidodynamic extreme, the metadynamic is also paradynamic and epidynamic and protodynamic and parastatic and epistatic and protostatic. Each of us is identified with every ideology on the protostatic side of the most eidodynamic one implied by our behaviour, although it is this most eidodynamic one which determines our ideological classification.

Social Ideological Structure

The ideological structure of society is, in this respect, parallel with that of each person. In order to maintain expression of any ideology a society, like a person, must maintain expression of all those ideologies which lie to the protostatic side of it in the range. To show this for each ideology is a long, complicated and difficult task, and one which has not yet been carried out in full detail. ("The Enduring Eidostatics" goes some way toward establishing that the proto-, epi- and parastatic ideologies, and the groups identified with them, have to be accepted as functional constituents of any modern industrial or post-industrial society). Here we shall speak only in general terms, showing briefly the grounds for accepting that the general eidostatic phase is not, as it is sometimes thought to be, an obsolescent survival but has to be accepted as a functional constituent of any society which is to maintain the eidodynamic phase; we shall indicate the grounds for believing the conception of a purely eidodynamic society to be an illusion.

The eidostatic ideologies are negatively identified with the non-social world and the eidodynamic ideologies are negatively identified with the social world. Active concern with any object or class of objects, the impulse to work on it and establish or increase control over it, goes with negative identification with it. We find, accordingly, that the eidostatic ideological groups tend to direct their energies toward the non-social World; it is this world they regard as the source of the ills, the problems and difficulties from which we suffer, and it is this world they regard as needing attention.

The eidodynamics, on the contrary, display negative identification with the social world; it is this world they regard as the source of the ills, the problems and difficulties from which we suffer and it is therefore toward this world that their energies are directed.

A society which has its attention directed entirely outward toward the non-social world, an exclusively eidostatic society, may survive. A society which has its attention directed entirely toward its own structure, a purely eidodynamic society, cannot do so.

Every society, if it is to survive, must ensure that its people are fed. This requires the direction of energy and attention toward the natural, the non-social world, it requires eidostatic behaviour. If the people are to do more than barely survive then many other material commodities must also be provided, and all of them require, for their production, eidostatic behaviour. We can conceive of a society in which these activities would not be necessary, but as a practical matter, if we are concerned with the well-being of our children and our grandchildren and their immediate descendants, then we have to accept that most of the energy of our society, now and in the foreseeable future, will need to be directed toward the non-social world. This is to say that it will need to be expended in behaviour implying identification with the eidostatic ideologies.

These ideologies have to be accepted as functioning constituents of our society in the economic field. If our society is not to be a repressive one (and the eidodynamic assumptions exclude political repression) then those identified with these ideologies, now recognised as socially necessary, must be accorded means of expression for their assumptions in politics and in societal activities generally. We have to accept the continuing existence, in the political field and elsewhere, of eidostatic opinion in something like its present strength.

Conclusion

Let us assume the reader has found this outline sketch acceptable, that he has moved on to some of the studies which undertake to establish various parts of the theory and has found those also acceptable. Let us assume that he accepts, provisionally at least, the theory of systematic ideology. What effect will this have upon him personally? How will it influence his political views, his attitudes and expectations? It will produce a change more revolutionary than any he has previously experienced. He will not "change sides" as he may have done in the past. Instead, he will reject the conception of politics as a field in which one chooses a side, accepts this or that view and repudiates the others.

He will recognise that the field of ideology, and of social and political belief and action connected with ideology, is not a field which is dominated by arbitrary subjective choice. Neither is it a mere reflection or superstructure, governed by the events occurring in some other field; ideology is not merely an epiphenomenon of economic processes. Ideology is, like economics, psychology, biology and other such fields, a relatively independent area. It exhibits phenomena peculiar to itself, entities and events which are systematically related one to another, and processes which follow recognisable laws. All of these require, for their full comprehension, study of the internal relationships of the field itself, as well as study of the influence exercised by adjoining fields.

The study of ideology is still in a very early phase; the systematic ideologist is still able, for the most part, to speak only in general terms, and there are wide areas of activity which have not yet undergone even a preliminary ideological survey. But one conclusion which has been solidly established, receiving further confirmation from each study of particular areas, is the presence in our society of an ideological structure, exercising an influence which is not yet generally recognised.

I have tried to outline this structure, presenting, very briefly, each of the major ideologies, mentioning some of the more significant relationships between them and indicating that there is reason to regard each of them as a necessary functional constituent of modern industrial or post-industrial society. In the broadest terms, a society which is to endure must be supplied and maintained, and with these functions the eidostatics are concerned. If the society is to endure in the face of accelerating technological development then it must not only be supplied and maintained, it must also be constantly reformed and, on occasion, revolutionised, and with this the eidodynamics are concerned. If a modern society is to endure it needs eidostatics and eidodynamics, and when one enquires more closely then it is found that not only these two great ideological classes but also each one of the major ideologies is a necessary functional constituent of a modern society.

This is not generally recognised. Among all the different major political parties, movements, positions and theories there is not one which presents the others as being equally necessary with itself. Present systems of government vary, but they all have one thing in common. They all operate on the exclusive principle, they all assume that one ideology must prevail to the exclusion, more or less complete, of all others.

This assumption produces the greater part of the conflict, national and international, which not only deprives us of the benefits which modern society, with its productive systems, is capable of providing, but even puts our continued existence at risk. It does so because it ignores the ideological structure. The major ideologies, and the groups identified with them, being functionally necessary constituents of our society, cannot be eliminated. They can, for a time and to an extent, be suppressed, (at least in their overt political expression), but the effort involved produces stresses which become more unacceptable as our society becomes more integrated and the power of weapons increases.

The theory of systematic ideology indicates that we have to accept the range of major ideologies, and the groups identified with them, as enduring features of our society. This points to the conclusion that an adequate political structure would be one in accordance with the ideological structure, one which recognised that the major ideologies, and the major ideological groups, are complementary, rather than merely opposed, one to another. It is a conclusion which amounts to nothing more – and nothing less – than the recognition that if we are to survive we shall need to adapt our political system to the ideological realities.

In closing, let us recall what underlies the polysyllabic abstractions we have been using. "Ideological groups," "negative identifications," "economic individualism;" these, and similar terms, are only shorthand descriptions of ways in which people behave. It is people who form ideological groups, and it is people who form society and its ideological structure. When we speak of establishing a political system consonant with the ideological structure this is only to say that an adequate political system would be one that works with, and not against, the way in which people in our society behave.

Papers on Systematic Ideology

These papers all develop themes mentioned in this *Outline Sketch.* They can probably be obtained where you obtained this pamphlet; if not, then from the Walsby Society or from The Bookshop, [address]. They will be sent on request, but if you can enclose, for each paper required, two letterstamps, this will be helpful[1].

The Ideology of a Monument. A Commentary on "The Monument. The Story of the Socialist Party of Great Britain," by Robert Barltrop. (With some ideological remarks on the SPGB).

Rowan-Walford Correspondence. (John Rowan, a Humanistic Psychologist, sent George Walford a paper entitled "The Internal Society," with the jocular query as to how such an activity should be classified ideologically. The recipient, a heavy-minded type, chose to take the query seriously, and this is the resulting correspondence).

The Ideology of Freedom. A Commentary on *The Machinery of Freedom,* by David Friedman. (Mr. Friedman's book is an exposition of the theory of Anarcho-Capitalism).

Reply to a Socialist. (An ideologist replies to a letter from a Socialist saying that he feels bound to continue struggling against the present order of things, whether or not his struggles are successful).

The Ideology of Ecology. A Commentary on *Manifesto for a Sustainable Society,* issued by The Ecology Party.

The Transparent Mask of Marxism. (Notes on the relevance of ideology to the structure and functioning of the Marxist movement).

In Defence of Ideology. (A reply to the charge that thinking affected by ideology is *ipso facto* invalidated).

The Enduring Eidostatics (A demonstration that the eidostatic ideologies, and the groups identified with them, are necessary functional constituents of modern society).

---

[1]These papers, and many more, can be found at the publisher's website: gwiep.net

Notes on the Ideology of Economics. Part One: Control of the Means of Production. (This paper sets out to show that common ownership and democratic control, and private ownership and autocratic control, of the means of production are not, as they are commonly assumed to be, mutually exclusive, but complementary).

The Domain of Ideologies, by Harold Walsby. (This book is the fundamental work on systematic ideology. Arrangements are being made for it to be reprinted. Price not yet fixed).

If you would like to be kept informed of developments in systematic ideology, or of the meetings and other activities of The Walsby Society, please contact the source from which you obtained this pamphlet, or write to The Bookshop, [address].

Select Reviews

Chronological excerpts from select reviews of
Beyond Politics.

– Trevor Blake

Systematic ideology has been defined as "the ideology of ideology." That this definition was provided, not by George Walford, but by an early reader of his book, Thelma Shinn, of the State University of Arizona, supports Mr. Walford's contention that s.i. – as we call it in the trade – is very much an evolving subject, since the book itself has no such succinct definition. A moment's reflection will show the width of the gap that has now been plugged. [...] S.i., I have observed, offends some because it seems formulaic and deterministic. Yet few would deny that society has built-in rules: bankers and insurance companies depend mainly on rules-of-thumb. The need, then, in dealing with Mr. Walford's theses, is not, it seems to me, to criticise them from afar, but to see whether they meet, item by political item, the Popperian test. Nobody, I can affirm, would welcome this more than the author.

George Hay
Science & Public Policy
Volume 17 Number 5
October 1990

Every anarchist should read this book. It is neither an essay in anarchist propaganda nor a put-down of anarchism, but a presentation of anarchism in a thoroughly unfamiliar light. The erudition leaves you gasping. The lucid, witty style is a delight in itself. And it makes you think, which is always a healthy exercise.

DR[1]
Freedom, the anarchist fortnightly
circa 1990

---

[1] possibly Donald Rooum - publisher.

214

This is a readable and thought-provoking little book. While many people have come to somewhat differing conclusions as a result of their own studies and speculation, I am sure they will find interest and mental stimulation in following George Walford's carefully evolved argument. [...] I enjoyed following the entwined arguments of this book, often in accord but sometimes questioning or disagreeing. I could not, for instance, accept his final conclusion that the emergence of the study of ideology marks a point beyond which further major ideologies are unlikely to appear. In conclusion I will say that the book provoked thought and that in itself made it enjoyable.

Ailsa Pain
PLAN, Journal of the Progressive League
November 1990

This is a book about ideologies. An ideology is a way of seeing the world, a more or less coherent philosophy of the way things seem to us to be. Walford is saying here that this is a valid and interesting phenomenon, which deserves more and better study than it has often had. He adopts the theory of systematic ideology first put forward by Harold Walsby, which says that there are very few ideologies, and that they are permanent. Thus there is no way of eliminating an ideology which we may dislike, and no possibility of humanity evolving beyond the existing set of ideologies. [...] This is a very stimulating and important book, which has much in it which must be read by anyone interested in this subject, but it would be much better if it somehow did more justice to the insights and the researches of feminism.

John Rowan
Self and Society, European Journal of Humanistic Psychology
Vol. XVIII No. 6
November / December 1990

I read this book with great interest and pleasure. The clarity of Walford's prose and the logic of his explanation of systematic ideology provide an excellent foundation for further exploration. While Walford's division of the six ideologies he identifies into the eidostatic and the eidodynamic owes a debt to Mannheim's *Ideology and Utopia* divisions, the recognition that ideology underlies much more than either politics or even the sociology of knowledge carries his thesis far beyond Mannheim's emphasis on ideological distortions and limitations. [...] What I found particularly rewarding about the book was that even the effect of his own attachment to a set of assumptions which inevitably govern his analysis is accounted for by the larger framework in which he establishes the outline of systematic ideology. There has always been a concern that society cannot be objectively examined because of the involvement of the observer in what is being observed, but quantum theory has made us aware that the same is true of the scientific examination of the physical universe. Walford acknowledges when discussing the ideology of principle that categorization must always involve "fuzzy edges and internal irregularities" but can be "none the less put to fruitful use, in serious study as well as in everyday life."

Thelma J. Shinn
Ethical Record
February 1991

Everybody has emotions about politics. Sometimes we give voice to them: public figures, like Norman Tebbitt and Nicholas Ridley, with great publicity and considerable consequences. Many of us also support a party and vote for it. We know, or think we know, what these parties stand for, at least on the one point that really matters to us or gets our goat. But have we really read their programmes, understood what they say and, more important, unravelled what they don't say but will do, after we have voted them into power on those points they have made publicly, and which we think we have understood? And how many of us truly know and understand what these parties really stand for, the thinking behind their thinking, and how far this thinking has been – can be! – translated into reality? George Walford – a longstanding subscriber to *Clarity*... has devoted many years to the study of this question. [...] Politics rule our life. They are behind the laws that govern what we may do and not do. And ideology is the conscious, or unconscious, system of assumptions behind our political views. The book is clearly and competently written and free from the emotional posturing so often found in political books. [...] You may have certain political attitudes. If you wish to know why you hold them, read this book.

Charles Sprague
Clarity, Magazine of the Christian Forum
Vol 22 No. 5
March 1991

The emergence of this book suggests that grand narrative in the human sciences lives on, despite the attempts of post-modernists to sign its death warrant. For Walford contends that ideology forms part of an evolutionary continuum that begins with atoms and ascends though 'molecules, single cells, multi-cellular creatures, human beings, ideological groups, and the societies they constitute.' 'Systematic ideology,' he believes, can plumb these depths and it thus holds the key to all past and future social development. In this analysis, ideology does indeed go 'beyond politics.' [...] *Beyond Politics* is dense and over-ambitious. It is also somewhat immodest. Thus Walford asserts that all future ideological developments following the advent of 'systematic ideology' will be variations on the themes of the major ideologies he has considered. While it may be true that innovation will take this restricted form, the determining influence of 'systematic ideology' is not so clear. Walford also overestimates the longevity of ideology: reducing it to primitive impulses obscures both its historical and epistemological specificity. His discussion of ideology in relation to the development of organic and inorganic matter is also unhelpful. One is left with the feeling that the book's underlying polemic against 'eidodynamism' could have been waged to greater effect without being made to carry quite so much excess evolutionary and terminological baggage.

Julia Stapleton
Durham University Journal
July 1991

It gives me no pleasure to pronounce this book mere drivel because every effort to understand and deal with the mess that the world is in should be encouraged. The conclusion is easy to come to because it is clearly written, unlike much academic drivel which is being pumped out of the universities in wilfully obscurantist form. Why do people believe what they do, and what causes them to change their mind? For the day-to-day struggle, getting in the necessities of life, i.e. material considerations is the spur. For changing the world, it is clearly not enough. A book is needed but George Walford's is not the one.

Ken Smith
Spanner
No. 4
February 1993

George Walford has contributed articles on anarchism and related issues to both *Freedom* and *The Raven,* and regularly features in *Freedom*'s correspondence columns. Much of his arguments and ideas in these pieces derive from his exposition of 'systematic ideology,' which attempts to examine and explain 'ideology' and which argument he develops to some length in his book *Beyond Politics* [...] Walford's book is an interesting read and does explain what an 'ideology' is. However, life and ideas do not fall into the tidy patterns he sees and there is definitely much in this work that anarchists will disagree with.

Jonathan Simcock
Freedom
May 1993

Jack as I Knew Him

by Alison Walford, Sharon Goodyer and Richenda Walford

GEORGE had a happy secure childhood up to the age of ten. He said his mother was always there, good-tempered and understanding, while his father, a self-employed workaholic builder, put in brief appearances during which George learnt roller-skating, cycling and swimming; it was the foundation for a lifetime's interest in individual sports. For several years his mother was ill, then she died of cancer in 1929. A very capable, jolly aunt, the father's sister, had offered to bring up George and his younger brother, Len, who had been born slightly brain-damaged, but his father refused.

Their father consigned the boys to a fee-paying orphanage, in Woodford, North London, owned and run by a fanatical, evangelical Baptist. This orphanage was run on the principle that "the Lord will provide," meaning that no appeals were made for food and clothing for the children. Prayers, grace and Bible study took up much of the children's day and in return The Lord was trusted to provide. Well, as George would say, "The Lord did not provide very much." George detested his time at the orphanage and had to work hard at overcoming his resultant repudiation of religion.

When George's father remarried five years later, his new wife, Edie Bailey, was eager to have the boys brought home, but the father resisted so strongly that a year-long battle had to be fought out before she finally triumphed. Edie welcomed the boys with little luxuries, such as a taxi ride and a visit to the theatre, and provided such a warm loving home that she won from George a deep, abiding affection.

George never forgave his father for that bitter, frustrating year waiting to be allowed home from the orphanage. For a time he worked unwillingly in his father's building business but quickly found a job he liked at the Mentmore pen factory, responsible for special orders. He had also tried to join the RAF; he wanted to fly, but was turned down on bad eyesight.

George's spare time was packed with activities: sports, visiting the opera and learning languages. It was at the Linguist Club that George met a German refugee who introduced him to anarchism. In a Soho cafe called the Coffee An' he met Ike Benjamin and other members of the Stepney branch of the SPGB, and Harold Walsby. All the time he was reading and studying (using his lunch money for books). Not carrying any of the baggage that came with a secondary education his mind was clear for reception and rejection of ideas; all were considered.

But it was not to last. War came and George registered as a political conscientious objector. He was directed to do non-combatant work for the armed forces. He would not do this; he obtained false identity papers and went on the run. For a time it was quite exciting, but not being registered for employment he could only make a living on commission work which was mainly door-to-door selling in provincial cities. In Glasgow he got a job as fire-watcher at a newly opened arts club called "The Centre," in Scott Street, close to the Glasgow School of Art. David Archer, a patron of young unpublished poets and a former Soho habitue, was its founder and benefactor. Here for the first time in his life George got to know artists, musicians and poets. He met established painters like Yankel Adler, Josef Herman and J. D. Ferguson, as well as young art students, like Alison McIntosh, whom he was later to marry.

As children, Sharon and Richenda heard their mother call their father "Jack" and believed that this was an affectionate version of "George." Only later in life did they discover that she had first met him as "Jack Hyams," his alias while on the run during the war – such romance! The poet, Sydney Graham, helped George with poetry composition. For a while George thought he was going to be a poet and throughout his life he read for relaxation: Milton, Kipling, Auden, Thomas Hardy and others. To our delight he often recited passages and apt quotations would be dropped unexpectedly into the conversation.

By nature George was a risk-taker, but his abstract thinking sometimes overrode the necessity to take suitable precautions. The authorities caught up with him and he landed in Barlinnie jail for three months. After release he still refused to comply with directives and carelessly found himself in prison again, this time in Wandsworth. However he made good use of this "time" by making a study of Shakespeare's plays. Afterwards, drawing a comparison between the two establishments, it appeared Barlinnie was to be preferred, scrupulously clean, with a firm, strict regime, whereas Wandsworth was dirty, relaxed and badly organised.

He remained in London after he was released and along with Walsby and several others became engaged in organising a group called the Social Science Association of which he was secretary. It was in this capacity that he contacted George Orwell and was invited to tea, although nothing much came of the meeting. George was never a socialiser; small talk was anathema. The SSA published several pamphlets and when the atom bomb was dropped they worked day and night to get out a pamphlet that was the first publication on sale devoted entirely to the atom bomb. Through a contact of Walsby's they got it distributed through W. H. Smith's shops and bookstalls where it sold very well.

A short time after the war ended Walsby happened to be asked by his friend, David Low an antiquarian bookseller, if he could recommend a suitable young man as an assistant in his business. George was recommended and accepted. This job proved to be a turning point in his life. He thoroughly enjoyed the work and it was not long before he set up in business on his own account. Marriage followed and he and Alison were soon fully occupied running a business and bringing up their two daughters, Sharon and Richenda. George maintained his interest in ideology but he had to suspend his activities in this field for some years. Never an idler, George worked long hours for many years, proving himself an astute businessman. He worried endlessly over each decision but the business was successful. His son-in-law, Nicholas Goodyer, joined him and gradually took over the management of the business, thus providing George with the freedom to continue his ideology activities.

The children's interests enabled him to continue his outdoor activities; swimming, riding, etc. and after they grew up he went on to sub-aqua diving, then yachting and sailboarding. He went skiing a number of times with Sharon and Nicholas but this was curtailed by the arrival of their children, Catherine and Richard. For several years George spent most weekends sailing the Channel, to the Isle of Wight, the Channel Islands and France, and on long summer holidays he made several trips to the Azores, usually single-handed, with no radio. He was also taking risks with hang-gliding, but gave that up after breaking his arm by falling onto the top of a Welsh mountain. He learnt to fly a Cessna and held a light aircraft pilot's license but found flying an aeroplane "a very dull experience." Of all the sports he enjoyed the sea was his great love and up to the end of his life he was sail-boarding in Portland Harbour. Latterly he had taken up hill walking with a group of friends including his sister-in-law, Brenda.

When he first met Harold Walsby, George was a member of the SPGB and initially he argued against Walsby's theory of ideology. As George said later "I went into Coffee An' one night wearing my intellectual SPGB bovver boots and came out battered, beaten, bemused and bewildered." George was quickly converted and over many years worked with Walsby, following him into and out of Hegel. Walsby died in 1973; for some time he had produced no new writing, but was taken up with algebra. George may have found this frustrating; certainly it was after Walsby's death that he returned to his work with systematic ideology.

Progress in thinking about systematic ideology can be charted in George's journal, *Ideological Commentary*, and also in his three published books. Great help at this time came from Richenda, a professional computer manager who provided invaluable advice, initially in a computer system for the business and then in word processing. George was quick to spot technological advances that would enhance his ability to put his ideas across and was soon able to advise the expert in her own field!

A brief word about George's health; he was slim, fit and lively but, in fact, was none too healthy. From his early years he knew he had a duodenal ulcer. He was often very ill and his life was punctuated with four major operations. The condition controlled his entire manner of living, especially eating and traveling. But in the end it was his heart which dealt the final blow.

George's family miss him greatly, as a role model of hard work and achievement, as a source of knowledge and wisdom but mainly as someone with whom to share life, laughter and love.

NIAT – Nothing Is Absolutely True

Index

Additional Reading in Systematic Ideology

The Domain of Ideologies by Harold Walsby

A study of the development and structure of ideologies. The foundation document of the study now known as systematic ideology. Familiarity with the *Domain of Ideologies* is essential for a thorough grasp of the theory and the changes it has undergone since inception. One of the most important contributions to the development of a scientific treatment of man's social and political consciousness. New edition with bibliography, index, reviews, criticisms and afterword.

gwiep.net 2020
ISBN 978-1-944651-15-2

Angles on Anarchism by George Walford

Anarchists pride themselves on disagreeing with each other but most of them hold some ideas in common, for example that anarchism stands for freedom, has a special connection with the poor, and became a large movement in Spain; that it stands apart from all other movements; that it advocates a natural condition. And of course anarchists don't vote or form a party. *Angles on Anarchism* challenges every one of these beliefs. New edition with introduction, reviews, index and criticisms.

gwiep.net 2017
ISBN 978-1-944651-10-7

Ideological Commentary by George Walford (editor)

Ideological Commentary was published in sixty-four issues by George Walford between 1979 and 1994, and was an independent journal of systematic ideology. It was published in London, England.

The Bookshop
ISSN 10960-8761

The Walford-Parker Exchange by George Walford and S. E. Parker

The Walford-Parker Exchange, originally published in *Ideological Commentary*, is gathered here for the first time with a new introduction. In one corner we have George Walford (1919 - 1994) representing systematic ideology, and in another corner Sidney E. Parker (1929 - 2012) representing Stirnerite egoism. Is egoism contradictory nonsense, or a self-evident description of the world? See these two articulate authors at odds in a friendly, informative exchange. New introduction by Trevor Blake

UnionofEgoists.com
Stand Alone 1035, 2017

The George Walford International Essay Prize

The George Walford International Essay Prize (GWIEP) is an annual essay competition in memory of the late George Walford. The subject of the essay is systematic ideology and the prize is £3,500 for the winner to spend at the college and on the course of his or her choice. Everything needed to apply for, research and win this prize can be found at no cost at this site. GWIEP is registered with The Charity Commission for England and Wales, number 1071002.

gwiep.net

9 781944 651237